ISRAEL

Promised Land to Modern State

ISRAEL

Promised Land to Modern State

by Rinna Samuel

VALLENTINE, MITCHELL · LONDON

First published in Great Britain 1971
by Vallentine, Mitchell & Co. Ltd.,
18, Cursitor Street, London E.C.4.

ISBN 0 853 03135 5

Reprinted in Great Britain by Lewis Reprints Limited
Port Talbot, Glamorgan
Bound in Great Britain by James Burn (Bookbinders) Limited
Royal Mills, Esher, Surrey

To my children, who are part of this story.

CONTENTS

ISRAEL

Promised Land to Modern State

In the Beginning

Someone once said that the Land of Israel suffers from too much history and too little geography, and there is much truth in this. Although Israel is only about the size of New Jersey, it has been the meeting place of East and West for more than five thousand years, the region from which sprang three great monotheistic religions that have had an enormous influence on mankind.

The State of Israel came into being in 1948, but its story actually has two beginnings. One took place halfway through the nineteenth century, when a movement arose among the Jewish people to resettle Palestine after two thousand years of exile; the other took place in the days of the Old Testament, for Israel is, above all, the Land of the Bible. Today, thanks to the many spectacular archaeological discoveries throughout the Middle East, we know that most of the Biblical stories are not simply legends or tales invented by a primitive people. Much of the Bible can be read, literally, as a history text. Most of the places it mentions really exist; the kings and prophets, heroes and heroines, leaders and generals, really lived; the events in their lives, their triumphs and tragedies, happened almost exactly as they are described in the Bible. And so, with the Bible as guide, we can go back across the centuries and trace the story of an ancient people who settled on an ancient land, who were forced to leave it, and then, hundreds of years later, returned to make it theirs again.

The Jews, first known as the Hebrews, came to Palestine around 1700 B.C. The Bible tells this story briefly and dramatically. A chieftain called Terah, his son Abraham, and the family left the village in which they had lived all their lives, a place known as Ur, on the banks of the Euphrates River, and set off with their flocks and chattel to look for a new home. They reached Haran in Upper Mesopotamia, and there Terah died. But after his father's death, Abraham wandered on. He explained that the Lord had spoken to him, saying, "Get thee from thy country, and from thy kindred, and from thy father's house, unto a land that I will show thee." Finally, Abraham reached that part of the Middle East which the Bible calls Canaan, and which much later was to be called Palestine, and there the Lord said to him, "Unto thy seed will I give this land." It was on the strength of this promise that Abraham and the weary, ragged herdsmen who had come with him from Mesopotamia settled in Canaan and made it their home.

When Abraham was a very old man in his nineties, God spoke to him again and repeated the promise: ". . . I will give unto thee, and to thy seed after thee . . . all of the land of Canaan for an everlasting possession and I will be their God." When Abraham asked the Lord for further assurances, the Bible tells us that God made a covenant with him and gave him the exact boundaries of the Promised Land "from the river of Egypt unto the great river, the river Euphrates."

Some hundred years passed, and drought and famine sorely afflicted Abraham's people. His grandson Jacob gathered them together and fled with them to Egypt, where they were enslaved, forced to do hard labor, and eventually threatened with death. In the thirteenth century B.C., a great leader arose

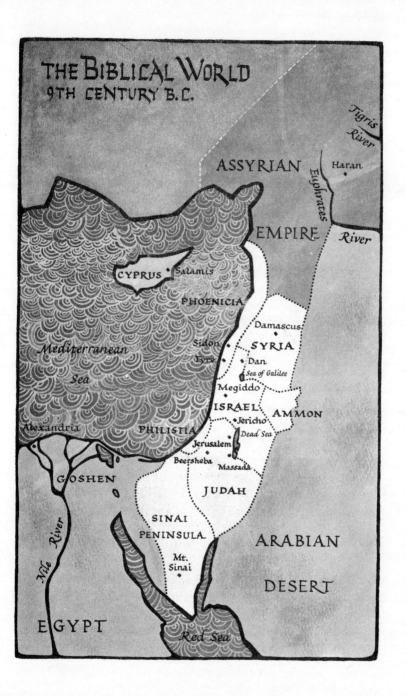

among Jacob's descendants, who were now organized into twelve tribes and called the Children of Israel: this was Moses, who united them and delivered them from oppression. He was a most gifted statesman and a very talented strategist. After many troubles and adventures, Moses led the Children of Israel out of Egypt, across the vast wilderness of Sinai back to the very frontiers of Canaan.

He did more, however, than lead the exodus of a persecuted people; in the desert, he made a nation of them. The Ten Commandments which, according to tradition, Moses received from God on Mount Sinai, and which were carved on stone tablets, were to be an important source of the laws which now govern human rights and duties in the western world. Not less important was the Law, the Torah, as it is known in Hebrew, which was in fact the code that gave the Jews specific rules and regulations as to how they were to farm, how they were to help the poor, how they were to marry and rear their children, how they were to treat their prisoners, what they were permitted to eat, and many other topics. It was not exactly a constitution, because the Jews believed that it was the sacred word of the Lord, but it dealt with both religious and secular matters and, in effect, defined an entire way of life.

To prepare the Children of Israel for the stresses and strains of their homecoming, Moses kept them wandering in the desert for forty years before he brought them to the borders of Canaan. He himself died within sight of the Promised Land, without ever entering it. But the twelve tribes, brilliantly commanded by Moses' lieutenant Joshua, crossed over the Jordan and, in a series of lightning campaigns, took the Land. It proved hard to hold. The people who surrounded it, the Moabites, the Ammonites, the Edomites, and, later, the Sea Peoples, the Philistines, fought and won back large stretches of it—from which it got the name of Palestine, or the Land of the Philistines, which it was to carry until 1948.

The Children of Israel, however, had one great advantage over their enemies. Bound by the ancient promise made to Abraham, united by their common faith and by the Torah, they fought hard, and Canaan was at last theirs. The Bible is full of colorful stories about these wars, defeats and victories, and about the extraordinary rulers which the small nation produced in response to these constant crises. The most famous king was a military genius. King David inflicted resounding defeats on the Philistines and expanded his kingdom until it reached the Red Sea in the south, and what are today called Syria and Lebanon in the north. Solomon, David's son, was primarily an administrator. Solomon turned Israel into a center of trade with Asia and Africa, and undertook enormous construction, mining, and transportation projects, making the most of the country's geographic situation. But by far the most lasting of his work was the building of the Temple. King David had made the city of Jerusalem his capital, and there Solomon erected the magnificent temple in which to house the holiest symbols of his people. It was to become a focal point of national unity.

The Hebrews fought a great deal among themselves, and around the tenth century B.C. they formed two separate kingdoms—Judah (from which comes the word "Jew") in the south of Palestine, and Israel in the north. Both these kingdoms were constantly threatened by the great and greedy empires of that period. The rulers of Egypt, Assyria, and Babylon all cast longing eyes on the Land and swore that, sooner or later, they would conquer it and subjugate its people. Confident that they had been chosen by the Lord for a special purpose, the population of the two kingdoms paid little attention to the various cultures around them and spent more time on internal quarrels than on preparing to face their enemies. From time to time, however, they gave way to the temptations of an easier and more relaxed way of life, and even turned away from the worship of the one God to pay tribute to alien deities.

15

One of the things which most sharply distinguished the Jews of Biblical days from all the nations around them was their great prophets—stern national commentators like Hosea and Amos in Israel, Micah and Isaiah in Judah, and, later, Jeremiah and Ezekiel. Essentially, the prophets were the guardians of the conscience of the people. Wise, fearless, and eloquent, they spoke frankly to the nation about those issues which affected everyone. In times of plenty, they warned grimly of the consequences of moral slackness, inequality, and injustice, and told the Hebrews that, unless they heeded the word of the Lord and obeyed the injunctions of the Torah, they would face disaster and even be sent away from the Land. In times of trouble, they comforted the people. They held up a vision of the time when "nation shall not lift up sword against nation" and again and again repeated that though they might be sorely punished, an immortal pact existed between the Jews and their God, and all the prophets stressed the special attachment of the People to the Land. The public often thought the prophets were demented, jeered at them, and sometimes drove them away, but their fiery words have rung through the centuries and are still part of the moral code of much of the world.

Then the dark days came and the most terrible of all the prophecies was fulfilled. The Kingdom of Israel fell to the mighty Assyrian Empire in 722 B.C.; the Kingdom of Judah was overrun by the armies of Nebuchadnezzar, ruler of Babylon. In 587 B.C., the beautiful temple in Jerusalem was destroyed and most of the population of Judah was killed. Those who survived were taken, in chains, as captives to a strange land. In Babylon, on the banks of the Euphrates, the Jews, as they were now known, went on studying their own laws, many of them dreaming of the Land they had left behind them. "If I forget thee, O, Jerusalem, let my right hand lose its cunning," they sang by the waters of Babylon It seemed as though the story that had started with Abraham had come to an end.

But the exile ended. In 539 B.C., Cyrus, King of the Medes and Persians, swept down on Babylon and crushed it. One of his first decrees proclaimed that the Jews could go home again—back to their own country. Judah was resettled and in 515 B.C. the Temple was rebuilt in Jerusalem on the site of the previous one. It was to stand for another six centuries.

The march of the great 'powers across the Land, however, went on long after the end of the Babylonian exile. After the Persians came the Greeks. In the beginning, Judah surrendered peacefully to the new rulers, but when Antiochus IV Epiphanes insisted that they worship Greek gods and goddesses, Jewish resistance stiffened. The king and his henchmen refused to accept the fact that this tiny people was willing to defy them, and decided to use force. The army of Antiochus IV occupied Jerusalem and desecrated the Temple, and the Jews were told they would be put to death unless they offered sacrifices to the foreign gods. The result was a wide-spread revolt led by one family—the Maccabees. Judas Maccabeus recaptured Jerusalem and cleansed the Temple and, after a period of guerilla warfare, the invaders withdrew from most of the country. But peace was not to return to the Jewish state.

After the Greeks came the Romans. For a while, the Romans set up a puppet kingdom called Judea under King Herod, in whose days Jesus was born in Bethlehem. Jesus lived and preached in Galilee and Jerusalem until A.D. 33, when, under the rule of the Roman governor Pontius Pilate, he was crucified in Jerusalem. His disciples, in particular Paul of Tarsus, undertook to spread the word of Jesus throughout the Roman Empire. Thus, the Holy Land became the cradle of a second international religion. When the Jews revolted against Roman rule in A.D. 66, the Romans invaded Judea outright. In A.D. 70, they razed the second Temple to the ground. Thousands of Jews were killed, and tens of thousands were ruthlessly taken prisoner and sold into slavery. Jerusalem was forbidden to the Jews and the country was given a new name: Syria

Palaestina. The Romans ruled with an iron hand, but small groups of Jews formed guerilla bands, and throughout Palestine rebellion broke out. The best-known of these uprisings, and perhaps the most tragic, was in a remote desert stronghold, overlooking the Dead Sea, called Massada. There, in A.D. 73 after years of siege, 960 Jews finally killed themselves rather than submit to the Romans. The last of these heroic insurrections was in A.D. 132, but the Roman legions of Emperor Hadrian crushed it within three years. Defeat was followed by a great slaughter, and the expulsion of the surviving Jews from Judea.

The Jews had lost the Land again. They were scattered throughout the vast Roman Empire, mostly among the lands which bordered the Mediterranean. Some went even further, into the eastern countries which were later to become Iraq and Iran. Others fled southward, into the distant and mysterious lands of Arabia, from which, two thousand years later, their descendants were to walk through the desert until they reached the giant transport planes that would fly them to the new Jewish state.

It seemed impossible that the Jews could continue to exist as a nation. They had no territory of their own, no political power at all, and were equipped only with an immense longing to return to Jerusalem and the conviction that, in the end, somehow or other they would do so. Because they were so sure of this, they determined, against all logic, to continue living as one people, despite the fact that they were so dispersed and had no national center. They created complicated rules and regulations with which to govern their day-to-day existence in the Diaspora, and these, it turned out, did in fact make it possible for the Jews to preserve their own way of life.

Most of all, they persisted in worshiping the one God in whom they believed, and to turn towards Jerusalem whenever and wherever they prayed. Each year, in their homes and in special schools, they read the Bible through from beginning to end, and its inspiring stories and poems sustained their hope that the time would come when God would bring them back to Israel. In fact, although many conquerors were still to covet and plunder the Holy Land, no other people ever attained independence there, or regarded living in it as the very reason for their existence. Some Jews still remained in Palestine, for the most part in old towns and small villages in the north of the country. But by the end of the first century A.D., the Land which Joshua had entered thirteen hundred years before was no longer the physical center of the Jewish people. The bonds between the people and the Land had taken new shape, one which no exile could—or did—break.

CHAPTER TWO

Next Year in Jerusalem

Exiled from the Holy Land, the Jews were a minority wherever they lived. At certain times and in certain places, such as Spain in the Middle Ages, they rose to positions of power and became important writers, doctors, and philosophers. A good example is Moses Maimonides, a Spanish Jew who lived in twelfth-century Egypt and who, in addition to being the leading scholar of the Jewish world, also became personal physician to the famous warrior Saladin and his court. But, for the most part, as the centuries passed the situation of the Jews darkened.

In Europe and in many of what are now the Arab states of the Middle East, they were forced to live in special sections of towns, often in walled-off compounds which were known as ghettos and which were locked at night, or in small, impoverished villages. In Russia, they were forbidden to live anywhere except in a specific area of the country, which was known as the Pale of Settlement. But even in more enlightened lands, in France, Italy, Germany, England, Poland, the Jews were badly treated, discriminated against, and very poor. In some places they were made to wear special clothes, and in others, an identifying badge on their sleeves.

Most ordinary forms of employment were forbidden them; they were not allowed to own any land, for instance, and there were virtually no Jewish farmers. They were not considered full citizens of the countries in which they lived, and for hundreds of years they were forced to earn their living as peddlers and petty tradesmen. Within their own communities, however, they maintained an almost perfect form of self-government, living by their own laws and religious rules, and taking care of each other. Since Hebrew was regarded as a sacred language and reserved for prayer and for the study of the Bible, the Jews created languages for everyday use. In Central and Eastern Europe, they spoke Yiddish, which was based on German, and in the countries along the Mediterranean, they used a language called Ladino which was based on medieval Spanish; both contained a large number of Hebrew words.

Although the way in which the Jews lived in the lands of the Dispersion seemed intolerable when looked at from the outside, in reality, by separating the Jews from everyone else, it strengthened them, taught them to endure, and made them rely on their own spiritual and intellectual resources. From time to time there would be a movement to return to the Holy Land, but none was ever successful.

For almost 2,000 years the Jews lived in this manner—and then, suddenly, the chains fell away. A series of massive social upheavals shook and permanently altered Western civilization, and changed the situation of the Jews. The French Revolution raised the stirring slogan of "Liberty, Equality, Fraternity," and, backed by the fury of a citizens' army and the determination of the French people to overthrow the rule of a privileged few, gave civil rights to the Jews of France. This was the beginning of a dazzling new freedom. The emancipation of the Jews spread to Belgium and to Germany, bringing the Jews there out of the darkness of the ghettos. In the bright sun of liberty, they rubbed their eyes and looked around them. It was as though they had been fossils, embedded in amber since the fall of Jerusalem, and now had been miraculously brought to life.

By the thousands, they rushed to take part in the opportunities for education and for non-religious culture; they learned the languages of the people around them, read the strange literature and poetry, and listened to the unfamiliar music. No longer was it necessary, they thought, to cling so strictly to their own ancient way of life. An entire world beckoned to them, and all of the delights of the late eighteenth and nineteenth centuries were theirs for the taking. Some Jews were drawn to the new, exciting political ideas of socialism and a classless society, and they, who had suffered so much and for so long, were ready to work for any cause that seemed likely to better man's condition.

Even in this brave new world, however, there were warnings that the position of the Jews was not altogether secure. Dislike and suspicion of them had certainly not disappeared, least of all in Russia—but there, too, underground tremors indicated the beginnings of some enormous social change. When it came, surely it would liberate not only the millions of serfs, but also Russia's large Jewish population.

In the meantime, many of the Jews in Europe, notably in France and the Austro-Hungarian Empire, took their place in the pleasant, graceful life of the continent's capitals. They became bankers and newspapermen and actors. The universities were open to them, and so were the free professions. Fewer and fewer Jews attended synagogues now, and more and more of them spoke German and French instead of Yiddish. They began to abandon many of their rituals, started to intermarry with non-Jews, and slowly drifted away from the traditions of the ghetto and its bitter memories.

One of the students who graduated from the law school of a European university in 1884 might have been taken as a symbol of the new Jew of Europe. Attractive and talented, he was not particularly concerned about what was happening to Jews elsewhere, and he was rather vague about the long span of Jewish history. It was impossible to foresee that this dapper young man, whose name was Theodor Herzl, would, within the space of only a few years, become the father of the first independent Jewish state since the destruction of the Temple.

Let us look at him more closely as he sips his coffee in one of Vienna's more fashionable cafes, humming a tune from a Wagnerian opera, talking about his prowess as a swordsman and his budding legal career, and about the few poems and plays he has written. His parents are worried because he seems not to have settled down yet, and he is already twenty-four. Money is not scarce in the Herzl family, but being an unsuccessful playwright with an eye for pretty girls is hardly a career in itself, and Herzl's father, himself a worldly businessman, feels that his son must start to make his own life. At the moment, though, beyond being slightly worried about his future, Theodor Herzl has no great problems. His parents have just sent him on a grand tour of Europe and now, as he lounges in the cafe, he decides that writing and traveling are the things he really likes best, and that he will go on doing them all his life.

It turned out that he did them both very well. After a while, he got a job on one of the most important Austrian newspapers, and eventually he was sent to Paris as a full-fledged foreign correspondent. In Paris, too, Herzl lived a glittering, easy, and interesting life; he wrote more plays, went to the theater a great deal, and mingled with sophisticated and creative people, not bothering about who was or who was not a Jew.

But this was not to last for very long.

Even in Paris, where Jews had now been free for a hundred years, anti-Semitism had not died. There is no reason to assume that Herzl wanted to ignore this unpleasant fact, but in any case the Dreyfus trial made it impossible for him to do so. This trial, one of the most dramatic ever to take place, was held in Paris in 1894.

Alfred Dreyfus, a Jewish captain serving with the French General Staff, was accused of spying for Germany and charged with treason. In actual fact, Dreyfus was quite innocent. The real spy was a Colonel Esterhazy, who had managed, together with some friends, to forge the papers upon which the charge against Dreyfus was based. The court accepted Esterhazy's "evidence," and Dreyfus' decorations and epaulets were ripped off. He was publicly disgraced and sentenced to exile on Devil's Island, a terrible penal colony in French Guiana. Even from there, Dreyfus fought on to clear his name. Many of France's best-known writers, including Emile Zola, became deeply involved in the case, declaring that Captain Dreyfus had been made a scapegoat, not only for Esterhazy but for all of the pent-up anti-Jewish feeling of the French army.

Dreyfus was finally freed, but for Herzl the screams of the mob demanding the captain's disgrace and death served as a funeral dirge for the hopes of all the Jews of Europe, himself included. The dream of real equality lay shattered. If this could happen in enlightened Paris, he felt, then it could happen everywhere else; the emancipation had failed.

As he covered the Dreyfus trial for his newspaper, Herzl came to realize that even if the ghetto walls had become invisible, they still stood, a permanent barrier between the Jews and the rest of the world. There was only one solution; it was a dramatic but logical one. The Jewish people must find a home of their own, one place in the world which would be theirs by right.

He expanded this wild idea in a book, *The Jewish State,* which he published in 1896. Herzl believed he had laid down the guiding principles of a theory the world would at first consider insane. He put aside his work as a foreign correspondent, forgot about tennis and concerts, and began to work in deadly earnest to organize the mass movement which he hoped would bring this state into being. Neglecting his wife and children, ignoring his old friends, he set out on the crusade which was to take up all his time and energy for the next eight years.

"I am profoundly convinced that I am right," he wrote, "though I doubt whether I shall live to see myself proved so . . . it depends on the Jews themselves whether this political document remains for the present a political romance. If this generation is too dull to understand it rightly, a future, finer, more advanced generation will arise to comprehend it. The Jews who will it, shall achieve their State."

In his book, which was read by few people, Herzl lamented the fact that the Christian world had not really accepted the Jews as equals after all; this was, he said, because the Jews had not presented themselves as a nation among nations. Only when they had done this would persecution end. Through what he called "the long night of their history" the Jews had dreamed of a Return. "Next Year in Jerusalem is our age-old motto," he wrote. "It is now a matter of showing that the vague dream can be transformed into a clear . . . idea."

Herzl worked out the most minute details of his plan. Large numbers of Jews should set out immediately for the new state, a militia must be created to defend it, and small houses must be built at once for the manual workers who should be among the first to arrive. He made a timetable which stipulated exactly at what stage the intellectuals and white-collar workers should join their comrades in the Jewish republic, and even concerned himself with such problems as the kind of flag to be designed, the languages to be spoken, and the amount of money to be paid to each worker. He also suggested that two organizations be created to take care of the essential formalities. The first of these was to be a "Society of the Jews" which would represent and negotiate for everyone, and the other he described as "a Jewish

Company" to be responsible for the raising and spending of the immense sums of money that would be necessary to translate his vision into reality.

At first, Herzl was not sure just where this Jewish state should be located. For a while he toyed with the idea of placing it in the Argentine, but then he became convinced that only Palestine, to which the Jews were bound in so many emotional and historical ways, could serve the purpose. One of the most interesting things about this remarkable man was the fact that he knew very little about similar ideas that were percolating far away from the boulevards and coffee houses of Paris. But, as often happens in history, the same drama was enacted in different ways on different stages. Herzl's basic idea was already under intense discussion in Russia, which had been virtually untouched by the emancipation that swept Western Europe.

The conditions under which Jews were forced to live in Russia had always been among the worst in the world, and now they faced increasingly cruel restrictions. Cossack troops and peasants, with the clear approval of the government, made repeated and brutal attacks on entire Jewish villages. Some Russian Jews believed that, sooner or later, there was bound to be a revolution, and that it would bring complete liberation for the Jews as well as for the mass of Russian people. However, other Jews were not prepared to wait for revolution, nor did they believe that it would substantially change their situation. They, too, began to think in terms of Jewish independence, and came to the conclusion that somewhere in the world there must be one country which actually belonged to the Jews, a country in which Jews need not be a minority.

Throughout those sections of Russia in which Jews were permitted to live, small groups began to organize themselves under the name of "Lovers of Zion." The first of these associations was formed in 1881, fourteen years before Herzl's book was published, and its members started to leave for

Palestine at once. They arrived there equipped with little besides their determination and courage. To begin with, they would farm the land themselves, living a frontier life, regardless of its dangers, and thus they would reclaim Palestine. But, for the moment, Herzl knew virtually nothing of all this; he was lost in his own dream of the Jewish state, and in the creation of the political movement which he called Zionism.

CHAPTER THREE

THE LAND RECLAIMED

BURNING with his idea, Herzl set out to find people who would help him. He banged on doors, wrote letters, and pleaded for appointments with some of the greatest and most powerful men in Europe. He also made a plan for specific action, a plan so daring that it was unlikely to materialize. He would go to the Sultan of Turkey and ask for a charter permitting Palestine, which was then a dry, sparsely inhabited, and neglected province of the vast Turkish Empire, to be colonized by the Jews. In return, he would guarantee the Sultan enough money to pay all the debts of the magnificent but failing court in Constantinople. Herzl's friends were appalled; they tried to persuade him that this was out of the question, that the Sultan would never see him, that Herzl was in no position to make promises of any kind.

But Herzl persevered, and, through a complicated chain of well-placed connections, he actually got to Constantinople, where he spent several days in the hope of being presented to the Sultan. The mission was a failure, but Herzl was far from discouraged. The Sultan would see him yet. In the meantime, there were other things to do. One was urgent: the establishment of what he called a Zionist Congress, an assembly of representatives of those Jews who supported the idea of Zionism.

In the summer of 1897, the first Zionist Congress met in the Swiss city of Basle. Two hundred Zionists, most of them wearing full evening dress and white gloves to mark the solemnity of the occasion, gathered in the old Casino. They were an extraordinary collection of people, from every possible walk of life. Some of them were deeply religious; some were freethinkers and socialists. Among them was a professor of mathematics from Heidelberg, accompanied by six of his students; another was a famous author and specialist in nervous diseases. All they had in common was the fact that they were Jews and that, whatever misgivings they may have had about Theodor Herzl, they believed him to be a contemporary prophet.

To open the meeting, they rose to their feet and uttered the ancient Jewish prayer of gratitude, "Blessed art Thou, O Lord our God, King of the Universe, who has kept us alive and brought us to witness this day." Then they settled down to work. By the end of the day, they had compressed their entire program into a few words. Only its opening sentence really matters: "Zionism strives to create a home in Palestine for the Jewish people, which is secured by public law." The Congress also created a World Zionist Organization of which Herzl was, not surprisingly, elected president, and decided to put out a newspaper to publicize the cause. Although this odd meeting of a few cranks in Switzerland attracted little attention then, it was to have an explosive effect on subsequent world events.

It is time now to lower the curtain for a while on Herzl, and let the spotlight play on an altogether different part of the stage: on Palestine itself, and on what was happening there in the meantime.

The country to which those first pioneers from Czarist Russia came in the late 1800's had gone through alternate periods of great turbulence and relative tranquility ever since the fall of Jerusalem in A.D. 70. Empire after empire had battered its way across the Holy Land; the Crusades had stained it deeply with blood; it had been briefly in the uncertain possession of the Arabs, the Seljuks, and the Mamelukes; and now it was part of the Ottoman Empire. But in Jerusalem, Jesus had preached and died; Mohammed, so the Moslems believed, had ascended to heaven; and the Temple had once stood in the center of a Jewish homeland. No city in all of history had ever been so coveted, or conquered so often.

The Turks were perhaps the least interested of all the masters Palestine had known. For them, this was merely a territory they wanted no one else to have. They plundered the country for whatever it could yield, used its forests as firewood, let its topsoil be washed away, and the desert and the sea erode the land. They treated the Arabs who still lived there with contempt and cruelty, governing them with bribes and threats. They tried to profit from the trickle of pilgrims who came to pray at the holy places, and did nothing at all to develop the country in any way. In the four cities which were holy to Judaism—Jerusalem, Safad, Tiberias, and Hebron—there were, as there had always been, clusters of Jews, supported by charity and dedicated to the study of the Torah. But that was about all.

The first pioneering village was founded in 1878. It was called Petach Tikvah—the Gate of Hope—and it was established by three adventurous young men, one of whom had walked all the way from Hungary to Palestine with only a map of Asia and the equivalent of one dollar in his pocket. They put up tents and waited for more people to join them. The road to the colonies was paved with hardship; most of the Jews in Eastern and Central Europe were reluctant to help or encourage the young people who wanted to set out for the distant, trackless, waterless sands of a land they had never seen before, where they would surely perish, if not from thirst then from the whips of Turkish gendarmes. But somehow they found the rubles for the miserable journey across the borders of Europe to Trieste or Odessa, and for passage on one of the ships which plied the Mediterranean, stopping at Jaffa long enough to unload their weary human cargo. No one had asked the pioneers to come to Palestine and no one welcomed them. But they were strong, stubborn, and lit with an inner light that no amount of discomfort could put out.

The village of Petach Tikvah slowly turned into a small farming community; but life was not easy. One of the young pioneers who came to Palestine in those early years described, much later, his arrival in Petach Tikvah:

"The journey [from Jaffa] took three hours, and as there was no made-up road, the carriage often stuck in the sand. We passed many black Bedouin tents on the way, their owners standing beside them, holding rifles and revolvers. The countryside was open, empty and wide . . . Arabs, men and women, walked about the paths in the groves and from time to time a Jew rode among them on a horse or donkey. Then, we saw the white houses of Petach Tikvah. The carriage stopped in the middle of the settlement and we were immediately surrounded by a crowd of people wanting news and letters . . . young men were dancing in the street, and one of the new immigrants took a violin out of his luggage and began to accompany them. Soon, we were drawn into the circle of dancers. . . ."

The writer was the father of Israel's famous General Moshe Dayan.

Malaria plagued the settlers; the Yarkon River flooded its banks and took a toll of their meager property; the villagers had no idea how to behave towards the Arab peasants and no language in common with them. Often they thought they had made a dreadful mistake, but they hung on and eventually Petach Tikvah became an established community. Other Jewish colonies sprang up in its wake, all of them kept going by the same kind of determination that let nothing stand in its way—not the corrupt Turks, not the blisteringly long summers, not even the fact that the novice farmers hardly knew one end of a spade from the other.

These settlers were known as members of the "First Aliyah." The Hebrew word *Aliyah* means "ascent" or "going up"; in this case, going up to Zion from all corners of the earth and settling there. Although the aims of the First Aliyah were exalted, in actual practice the colonies were a far cry from the glorious Jewish state which the Zionists in Basle had envisioned. Altogether, there were about a thousand farming families. They spoke Yiddish or Russian, wore high-necked Russian blouses, and lived in shabby, badly built houses. They had learned something about agriculture, in particular about growing oranges, and had overcome the worst hazards of living in the new land. But was that enough? Even Herzl, who visited Petach Tikvah in 1898, came away depressed. It was a beginning, but something more was obviously needed if the Return were to be truly revolutionary.

The new ingredient was to be added in the course of a few years by another wave of pioneers, who became the "Second Aliyah." Analyzing what had gone wrong, they decided that settling in Palestine was not enough. The new way of life must be based on entirely new principles. The farm colonies must not become plantations depending largely on the work of hired help. All the members must live and work together, sharing in the fruits of their labor, and owning nothing privately. They called this new type of farm a *kibbutz*, from the Hebrew word for "group." They took the matter of self-reliance very seriously, and extended it to self-defense. They began to train themselves in the use of arms, to learn to ride horseback, to transform themselves into natives of the country.

And still the young men and women of the Second Aliyah were not satisfied. It was not enough to live in Palestine, or to farm it, even on a kibbutz. They wanted to use the language of their people again, to revive Hebrew as a spoken language. This presented a problem, for Hebrew had not been in daily use for nearly two thousand years. Could it, in fact, be dusted off, brushed up, and re-equipped for use in discussing the raising of poultry, or in naming the parts of a gun, or in teaching geography?

As it happened, among those who came to Palestine at the time of the Second Aliyah was Eliezer Ben Yehuda, who became known as the father of modern Hebrew. Long before this he had become obsessed with the idea that when the Jews returned to Palestine they must actually speak Hebrew, and not merely read and write it, as most pious Jews were able to do. He compiled a dictionary that he hoped would provide all the Hebrew words needed for modern living—including the word "dictionary" itself. When he married, he told his wife that, from that day on, no other language would cross his lips, and he kept his promise. Their son, born in 1882, was the first child in two thousand years to speak Hebrew as his mother tongue.

Ben Yehuda had a great influence on the young pioneers, and they followed his example. Now, to add to their difficulties, they forced themselves to speak only Hebrew. Great as the effort was, it helped make them feel involved in a history-making process, and reinforced the links of the ancient chain that bound them to their forefathers and to the Land.

In Europe, far from the heat, the mosquitoes, and the Arab marauders, Herzl continued to seek ways of getting his charter and raising money. Ceaselessly, he traveled through Europe, aware that his health was failing and that he might not live to see his Jewish state an established fact. At last the day came when he was to meet the Kaiser, through whom he hoped to make contact with the Turkish Sultan. Herzl saw the Kaiser three times, the first time in Constantinople itself in 1898. Wilhelm II was gracious but very brief.

"What do you want me to ask the Sultan?" he said.

"We want a chartered company under German protection."

The Kaiser said nothing more.

The second meeting took place that same year, in Palestine. It was Herzl's first visit to the Holy Land. On the grounds of an agricultural school established by the Jews in 1870 (the first of a series of such training centers for the new farmers), Herzl waited for His Imperial Majesty.

Later he described the meeting vividly:

"The highway was filled with a multitude of Arab beggars, women, children, and horsemen, to herald the approach of the Imperial train. Fierce Turkish cavalrymen galloped up at full tilt . . . then the European outriders. And finally— the Emperor himself . . . I stood at one of the ploughs and took off my sun helmet. The Emperor recognised me [and] held out his hand. He laughed and his imperious eyes flashed. . . .

" 'How has your Majesty's trip been so far?'

" 'Very hot. But the country has a future.'

" 'For the time being, it is still sick,' I said.

" 'It needs water, a lot of water,' he replied, '. . . It is a land of the future.'

"Finally, he held out his hand to me again, and trotted away. The Empress nodded and smiled. The Imperial train continued on its way."

This meeting also bore little fruit. Weeks afterward, in the scorching Indian summer of November in Palestine, Herzl was again received by the Kaiser, this time in a tent in the Holy City. Herzl read out the usual proclamation of greetings and respect. After a few courtesies and some small talk, the Kaiser of Imperial Germany and Theodor Herzl got down to business. They discussed the water problem once more, the health problem—and money. It was on this last point that the meeting broke up. The Emperor was sure Herzl had tremendous funds at his disposal, and he offered no concrete help. What of Imperial intervention with the Sultan? Well, it turned out that the Kaiser had already spoken to the Sultan about Herzl's charter, and the Sultan was not interested.

By 1901, none of Herzl's plans had materialized. The

Zionists were beginning to doubt his prophetic abilities. Perhaps, after all, his grandiose scheme was impossible to fulfill. Herzl suffered a heart attack. "I feel my autumn approaching," he wrote sadly in his diary. Then another avenue to the Sultan opened up, and at last Herzl was invited to meet the awesome Abdul Hamid, Sultan of the Turkish Empire, sole master of a crumbling but still great power.

Yes, Abdul Hamid would speak to his advisers, and yes, he would talk to the Chief Rabbi of Turkey. But for anything more, he would first have to see the money Herzl offered. How could it *possibly* be raised? The sum whispered by the courtiers in the silk-lined corridors of the palace was huge; thirty million pounds was the minimum that would solve the financial problems of the Ottoman Empire. It was out of the question.

Dejected and filled with rare self-doubts, Herzl left Constantinople. Perhaps the Jewish state could be located somewhere else, outside Palestine proper? There was the Sinai Peninsula—a great expanse of wilderness separating Biblical Canaan from Egypt. He rushed off to negotiate with British statesmen, but failed to win anyone over. Herzl finished the novel he was writing and called it *Old-New Land.* It was a description of the Jewish state-to-be and a pathetic though brilliant substitute for the real thing.

In Russia, the Jews were now gripped in a vise. In 1903, a frightful massacre took place and terror spread from one Jewish village to another. Perhaps the Czar of All The Russias would lend a hand to the creation of a state that might rid him of the despised, unwanted Jews. Herzl traveled to St. Petersburg to talk to the Czar's Minister of the Interior. He asked that the Czar see him, but was refused. He asked that the Czar intercede with the Turkish Sultan. The Minister said he would think about it. Herzl was desperate. The Jews of Russia must be saved.

An old, discarded suggestion suddenly re-emerged. What about Uganda, in British East Africa? It was virtually unpopulated, quite undeveloped; perhaps it would do. Herzl was prepared to try anything, but the Zionists rejected his proposal with some vehemence. They were not merely searching for an easy refuge; they wanted to reconstruct the Jewish commonwealth on the soil of the Land from which they had been expelled so long ago, and to which they had sworn to return. With tears in his eyes, Herzl begged his colleagues for permission to send a delegation to East Africa, at least to look around and examine the possibility of settlement. Unable to deny him entirely, the Zionists grudgingly agreed. But complications developed in the British Colonial Office and the Uganda scheme was shelved again. With an effort that was, literally, to cost him his life, Herzl attempted other solutions. He went to Italy, spoke to the King about settling the Jews in Tripoli, and tried to see the Pope. In May, 1904, he again fell ill, and by July, at the age of forty-four, he was dead.

All Jewry mourned him. He had failed, but he had shown the way; and now others would break the trail, if it was to be broken at all. Herzl was buried in Vienna. Today his remains, brought by an airplane flying the blue and white colors of Israel, lie on a hill bearing his name, in the city of Jerusalem—the capital of the Jewish state.

CHAPTER FOUR

THE RETURN

By 1914, on the eve of the First World War, there were 85,000 Jews in Palestine. The first all-Jewish city in the world had been established in 1909 on the sand dunes outside the ancient seaport of Jaffa. Its founders optimistically called it Tel Aviv—the Hill of Spring—and hoped that one day it would develop into a garden suburb, housing some sixty families. They named its first street after Herzl.

In the same year, the first collective settlement, or kibbutz, was created on the southern shores of the Sea of Galilee, on both sides of the Jordan River. Named *Degania*, "cornflower," it consisted of two primitive buildings, one very small farm, and fifteen members ranging in age from eighteen to twenty-five.

A self-defense organization, *Hashomer*—"The Watchman" —had been launched. It was the first military unit in modern Jewish history, and came into being primarily to guard Jewish property against Arab brigands. But it was more than just a collection of night watchmen. It was a group dedicated to discipline and self-sacrifice, a group determined to prepare itself for whatever the future might hold. Sitting on upturned wooden crates in a small lantern-lit hut among the orange groves that ringed Jaffa, a few young men solemnly undertook responsibility for the security of the pioneering community. Dressed in a combination of Bedouin and Russian clothes—flowing Arab headgear and high-necked Russian blouses—with bandoliers strung across their chests, the *Shomrim*, as they were called, pledged themselves also to do their utmost to develop friendly relations with their Arab neighbors while resisting the attacks of marauders. Eventually, the Arabs learned to admire the horsemanship and marksmanship—as well as the goodwill—of the Watchmen.

"All of us were new in the country," one of the Shomrim said later. "We felt as if we were standing before Mount Sinai at the giving of the Law, and we were ready for heavy sacrifices. Words and debates alone would not, we knew, build a nation."

The colonists hoped against hope that the war would pass them by, and, preoccupied in the struggle to keep going, they paid little attention to what was happening overseas. But as the war came closer to Palestine, Britain's interest in the Zionist idea deepened. A number of British statesmen began to show some curiosity about the possible usefulness of a tiny but active partner in their attempt to overthrow the Sick Old Man of Europe, as Turkey was then called, and assume supremacy in the Middle East themselves. One obvious ally was the Zionist movement.

Theodor Herzl had already made an impression in London, and the man who was to succeed him as leader of the World Zionist Organization was to make an even greater one. In 1906, Dr. Chaim Weizmann, a young Russian-born, Swiss-educated biochemist and a fervent Zionist, received a lectureship at the University of Manchester. He was a man of great charm, a scholar with access to intellectual circles, and he rapidly made contact with people who were able and willing to bring him close to the sources of influence in Great Britain. Perhaps the most important early connection Dr. Weizmann made was his meeting with Arthur James Balfour, the celebrated British statesman who had already been Prime

Minister and was now campaigning for election to Parliament. They met for the first time in an old-fashioned, dim hotel room in London. Balfour was famous, brilliant, languid, and worldly. Weizmann was young, new to Britain and to the ways of the British, not yet able to speak English fluently, and quite unknown to Balfour. Nonetheless, the Englishman was fascinated by him and asked many questions about the Zionist movement.

Balfour had heard of the ill-fated suggestion that Uganda be colonized by the Jews and told Weizmann that he thought something might still be done about it. Why *wouldn't* Uganda do? Weizmann tried to explain what Palestine meant to the Jews. Then, suddenly, he decided to say it very simply.

"Mr. Balfour," he said, "if I were to offer you Paris instead of London, would you take it?"

Balfour stopped lounging in his chair and sat up.

"But Dr. Weizmann, we *have* London."

"Ah, yes," replied Weizmann. "But, you see, Mr. Balfour, we had Jerusalem when London was just a marsh."

Balfour had never met a Jew who spoke in this manner. Dr. Weizmann's words jolted him, and he never forgot them. When the British Colonial Office began to swing in the direction of supporting Zionism, Weizmann was able to play a major, if not crucial, role.

By the time Turkey entered the war on Germany's side, the Jewish population of Palestine had been reduced to 56,000. The Turks, always hostile to the Zionists, were now more anxious than ever before to get rid of them. All the former Russian subjects were deported, including those who had taken out Turkish citizenship, and most of the founders of Tel Aviv. Worried that Hashomer might be the nucleus of a Jewish army, the Turks tortured and hanged many of its members. Hunger and disease struck the Jews remaining in Palestine. Farms began to fail for lack of men, and a typhoid epidemic broke out. It looked as though the young settlements would not endure, and the settlers became grim.

One of the extraordinary dramas of this desperate era was being enacted in the north of Palestine, in a settlement called Zichron Yaakov, where a secret group called *Nili* (an acronym of the Biblical phrase, "The Eternal One of Israel does not lie") was engaged in collecting information for the British. Nili was made up primarily of members of a fairly prosperous farming family, the Aaronsons. One of the Aaronson boys, Aaron, had achieved some degree of fame in agricultural circles as the man who had discovered true wild wheat, on the slopes of Mount Hermon, and as an expert on Palestine's wild life. He ran a small research station on the northern coast and traveled around the country a great deal. Convinced of the merits of the Allied cause, and anxious for a speedy Allied victory, Aaronson contacted the British headquarters in Cairo and offered to supply them with facts and figures which, he hoped, would be of military value.

With him worked his younger brother, several close friends, and his sister Sarah. The Jewish community knew about the Nili network and was terrified that the Turks would find out about it and execute or severely punish the participants. But the Aaronsons would not give up. Despite the danger and the fact that the British never acknowledged Nili's contribution, they continued their volunteer campaign of espionage.

Carrying out her part of the campaign, Sarah Aaronson went daily to the beach to wait for the small coaster which took the group's reports to headquarters in Egypt. One day, the Turks found a carrier pigeon with a message from Sarah to the British attached to its claw. The code in which her message was written was never broken, but it confirmed their suspicions. Ten days later, one of Sarah's comrades was caught by Bedouins near Beersheba and turned over to the authorities. Under torture, he verified the Turks' worst fears, and the noose tightened slowly around Nili's neck. Soon afterward, the little coaster appeared, accompanied this time by two small British warships, to evacuate the

members of the spy ring and their families. But Sarah refused to go; there was no need to panic, she said, and there
was still vital work to be done.

That same night, the Turks descended on Zichron Yaakov,
took Sarah into custody, and tortured her in an attempt to
make her confess. But young, blond, pretty Sarah was made
of unusually stern stuff. Rather than risk breaking under
torture, she shot herself. Her heroic suicide signaled the end
of the little band.

The idea of an active participation on the side of the
Allies expressed itself in many other ways. The idea spread that
the Jews must fight under their own flag, as a national entity.
A few hundred of the Jews who had been exiled from
Palestine and were now stranded in Egypt formed the first
unit. It was not allowed to take part in combat, and its
duties were limited to transport; it went into history under
the less than flattering name of "The Zion Mule Corps."

The Corps was led by a one-armed hero of the 1904 Russian war against Japan, a man called Joseph Trumpeldor,
who had been one of the few Jewish officers in the Czar's
army and who had come to Palestine for the specific purpose
of creating a Jewish army. Tall, slim, military in bearing,
Trumpeldor put his heart and soul into drilling the small
transport unit, and finally it served in the Gallipoli campaign, under heavy fire. The Corps was formed in 1915 and
disbanded after a year, but its veterans became the heart of
a real Jewish Legion, which eventually took part in the
British capture of the Holy Land, and which was made up of
a Palestinian battalion and one consisting of Jewish volunteers from the United States and the British Empire.

The Jewish Legion had its start in the Egyptian barracks
which had been given by the British to the Jewish refugees
from Palestine. One of the officers-to-be sketched the scene:

"About two hundred of us were present . . . we gave the
gathering a review of the position. Sooner or later, the British
forces would leave Egypt for Palestine. Bad news was ar-

riving daily from Jaffa . . . the Turks had declared that after the war they would not allow any Jewish colonization at all. That spring night, we signed a document on a piece of paper torn out of a child's exercise book. On it is written a resolution in Hebrew: 'To form a Jewish Legion and to propose to England that it be made use of in Palestine. . . .' "

Another piece of paper was to have an even more profound effect on developments in the Middle East. It was written on the stationery of the British Foreign Office and dated November 2, 1917—after the British Army had begun its Palestine campaign. Without any doubt, it is one of the most remarkable proclamations ever issued by any government. Its full text read:

Dear Lord Rothschild,
I have much pleasure in conveying to you, on behalf of His Majesty's Government, the following declaration of sympathy with Jewish Zionist aspirations which has been submitted to and approved by the Cabinet.

"His Majesty's Government view with favor the establishment in Palestine of a national home for the Jewish people, and will use their best endeavors to facilitate the achievement of this object, it being clearly understood that nothing shall be done which may prejudice the civil and religious rights of existing non-Jewish communities in Palestine, or the rights and political status enjoyed by Jews in any other country."

I should be grateful if you would bring this declaration to the knowledge of the Zionist Federation.

Yours sincerely,
Arthur James Balfour

The Balfour Declaration, sent to Lord Rothschild, who had submitted the official request, consisted of 67 words. It was curt, vague, and presented to the Jews something which the British did not yet possess and which still belonged to the Turkish Empire. But this curious document opened the way, at last, to the fulfillment of Herzl's dream.

The reasons for the British decision could be summed up as a combination of self-interest and a genuinely strong feeling that the Jews, victimized by history, deserved to return to their Land. Lloyd George was then Prime Minister of Great Britain, and had been raised on the Bible, as had many other British leaders of the day. For him and for Balfour himself, the Declaration had a singularly romantic meaning, the more so because within six weeks after it was issued the British Army, headed by General Allenby, formally received the keys of the Holy City. Jerusalem, evacuated by the Turks, was surrendered on December 11, 1917.

A year later, the First World War came to a halt. A Zionist Commission, headed by Chaim Weizmann, was sent to Palestine by the British Government early in 1918 to plan for implementation of the Balfour Declaration, and to examine the country's needs. Among other things, Dr. Weizmann met with Emir Feisal, the son of the Sherif Husein of Mecca whom the British had promised to make king of the Arab countries which had been liberated from Turkish rule. The two leaders met at the Red Sea port of Aqaba in the summer of 1918 and signed a pact of friendship.

In April of 1920 the Mandate for Palestine was formally given to Great Britain, later to be confirmed by the League of Nations. The military government of Palestine was replaced by a civil administration, and Sir Herbert Samuel, a British Jew of distinction who had been, in large measure, responsible for the Balfour Declaration, was appointed first British High Commissioner in Palestine.

For the first time in 1850 years, a Jew ruled over the Land of Israel, and the High Commissioner was received jubilantly. His first official visit, when he arrived in Jerusalem, was to the main synagogue in the Jewish quarter. It was on a Saturday, and to avoid offending the Orthodox Jews (to whom driving on the Sabbath is forbidden), Sir Herbert made his way on foot through the crowded, twisting alleys of the Old City. The service included the opening lines of a chapter of

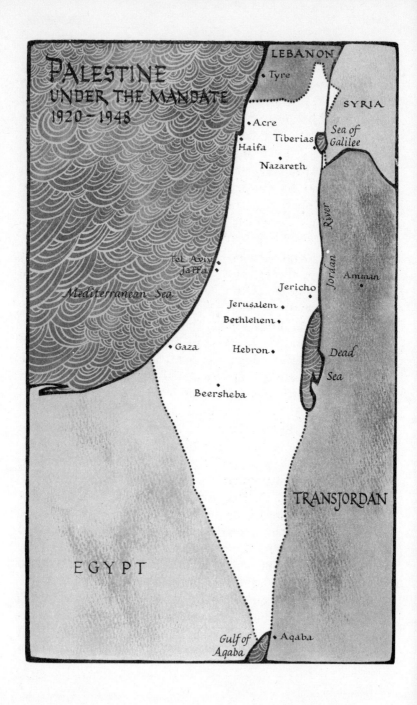

PALESTINE
UNDER THE MANDATE
1920 – 1948

LEBANON

• Tyre

SYRIA

• Acre

Tiberias
Sea of
Galilee

Haifa

• Nazareth

Mediterranean Sea

Tel Aviv
Jaffa

Jordan River

Jericho •

Amman •

Jerusalem •
Bethlehem •

• Gaza

Hebron •

Dead
Sea

• Beersheba

TRANSJORDAN

EGYPT

Gulf of
Aqaba

• Aqaba

Isaiah from the Old Testament: "Comfort ye, comfort ye, my people, saith your God. Speak ye comfortably to Jerusalem and cry unto her, that her warfare is accomplished, that her iniquity is pardoned." Long afterwards, the High Commissioner wrote of that morning, "The emotion that I could not help but feel seemed to spread through the vast congregation. Many wept. One could almost hear the sigh of generations."

But Jerusalem's travails were far from ended. In their eagerness to strengthen their position in the Middle East, the British and the French had carved up almost all of the former Turkish Empire and apportioned it among themselves. This despite the British negotiations with Sherif Husein and the promises they had made to him. Instead of being given immediate independence, the Arab states were parceled out as mandatory territories, to be governed by France and Britain on behalf of the League of Nations. In their fury at what they considered British duplicity, the Arabs made an issue of Palestine.

Even though, initially, both the Jews and the Arabs understood that the Balfour Declaration excluded Palestine from any area of Arab sovereignty, and despite the Weizmann-Feisal agreement, the Arabs now claimed that here, too, they had been betrayed. The ambiguity of the Declaration added to the confusion. What, exactly, was meant by a "national home for the Jewish people"? What were Britain's real intentions? Hadn't Palestine been pledged to the Arabs as well?

Palestine now became the much-promised land ·in Arab eyes, and the focal point of their grievances. Nonetheless, for about seven years there was relative peace and quiet in the Holy Land. From time to time Arab extremists incited the peasants to attack the Jews, telling them that their land would be taken away from them and turned over to infidels from the West. In one such Arab attack on a Jewish settlement, called Tel Hai, in the north of Palestine, Joseph

45

Trumpeldor was killed. Responding to the settlement's appeal for help, Trumpeldor and a group of Jews from the south rushed to Tel Hai with arms and food. They found it surrounded by thousands of armed Arabs. In the ensuing battle, Trumpeldor was mortally wounded. As dusk fell, he died; with his last breath he whispered: "Never mind. It is good to die for our country." The defense of Tel Hai became both a portent of the future, and a symbol of resistance for the new generation of Jews growing up in Palestine.

In spite of occasional Arab riots, the Jews continued to develop their own economy, educational system, and agriculture. Gradually, under their intensive care, the desert was pushed back and Palestine started to become green again— as it had once been. From 1919 to 1924, nearly 50,000 immigrants arrived in Palestine. Many went into the cooperative farms and collective settlements; they built roads, drained swamps, and readied the land for settlement. Others worked in the building trades, and helped turn Tel Aviv, which had already grown far beyond its founders' dreams, into a fair-sized town. By the end of 1925, Tel Aviv had a population of 40,000.

Along with agriculture, which was the pioneers' main concern, industry also developed. A Russian Jew who had worked for the creation of the Jewish Legion devised a plan for the electrification of Palestine, and built a power station in Tel Aviv. A salt factory, an oil refinery, and a flour mill were in operation by 1925, and a number of small industrial plants were established.

The small Jewish community also ensured its intellectual future. A high school was built in Tel Aviv, a technological institute was opened in Haifa, and Lord Balfour himself came from England to attend the dedication of a Hebrew university on Mount Scopus, in Jerusalem. From this hill all of Jerusalem could be seen on the one side, while on the other lay the lovely landscape of the Jordan Valley and the Dead Sea, with the lavender-misted Moab Mountains in the background.

Twelve thousand people listened to Balfour's magnificent speech. Standing before the crowd in his bright red academic robes, his white hair blowing in the wind, Balfour looked less like a British elder statesman than like a Biblical prophet. The world might scoff at the audacity of opening a university whose student body numbered all of 164, and critics of the idea might demand to know why young Palestinian Jews could not study abroad. But Dr. Weizmann, a major architect of Jewish higher education in Palestine, speaking on behalf of the Zionist movement, patiently explained that the fledgling university was no less important to the Jewish homeland than draining the thousands of acres of swampland bought from Arabs, or the creation of dozens of cooperative villages which had come about since the end of the war.

Meanwhile, Herzl's "Jewish Company" had become the Jewish National Fund, which bought land in Palestine in the name of the entire Jewish people. A third Aliyah brought some ten thousand new immigrants to Israel each year. For the most part, they too were from Russia and Poland. In all respects they were ideal pioneers—young, energetic, and well aware of the task that lay before them. If anyone could plant trees, produce successful farms, and raise crops in this singularly thankless land, it was these tough young men and women.

Not to be overlooked as an additional cause for optimism was a resolution passed by the United States Senate and House of Representatives in 1922 which placed on record that "the United States of America favors the establishment in Palestine of a national home for the Jewish people." It was signed by President Harding.

Although the Arabs rumbled, and the British seemed reluctant to take a forceful stand against their periodic attacks on the Jews, the 1920's nonetheless witnessed relative peace in Palestine—certainly compared with what was to come. And the record of achievement by far surpassed the dreams of the first pioneers. What in 1909 had still been highly experimental was an established reality by 1925. The resettlement of Palestine by the Jews attracted worldwide attention, particularly to their spectacular reclamation of the land. The Permanent Mandates Commission of the League of Nations, not given, as a rule, to lyric statements, described what was taking place there as "the greatest colonizing enterprise of modern times," and in London, Winston Churchill declared that the Jewish efforts in Palestine were "a great event in the world's destiny."

CHAPTER FIVE

Refugees, Riots
and Restrictions

Early on Monday morning, February 19, 1934, forty-three boys and girls, all German citizens, arrived in the port of Haifa aboard the *S.S. Martha Washington*. They ranged in age from about fifteen to seventeen. They were well-dressed, well-fed, healthy (except for a couple of sore throats and one bad cold, dutifully listed in the ship's log), and visibly eager for the adventure which lay ahead. Their names were uniformly German: Inge, Siegfried, Gerda, Fritz, and even an Adolf. They were, in the main, fair-haired, blue-eyed, and pink-cheeked; and the only language they knew was German. It is doubtful whether they understood exactly what it was that they had been rescued from. But it is quite certain that on this chilly early spring morning in Palestine, neither they nor the small reception committee that waited on the windy dock to welcome them could possibly imagine the extent of the horror that was to erupt in the country these children had left only a few days before.

These were the first young people to be brought to Palestine by a remarkable organization called *Youth Aliyah*. They would be followed in the years to come by thousands of hungry, tired, orphaned children, gathered up first from Germany and then from the rest of Hitler-held Europe, and taken to an uneasy haven in Palestine. *Youth Aliyah* means the Ascent of the Children, and this is as good a place as any to start the story of the greatest disaster ever to befall the Jewish people, and what the little Jewish community in Palestine did about it.

The long shadow of Nazism began to slant across Germany in the early 1930's. After the catastrophe of the First World War, an impoverished and bitter Germany found inspiration and hope for the future in the grandiose social and political programs formulated by the National Socialist Party, which was led by an unbalanced, crafty young Austrian called Adolf Hitler. Calling upon the Germans to restore Germany to her former glory, Adolf Hitler hit upon a singularly successful method of persuading them that nothing could stand in their way. They were, he told the Germans over and over again, a master race. They were proud Aryans whose downfall had been brought about, in large measure, by the Jews, to whom they had surrendered their economy, their cultural traditions, and, indeed, their national integrity. In the course of time, Hitler was to find other scapegoats as well, and to turn against all those elements in German society which dared oppose him. Even so, the extermination of the Jews would remain one of his principal aims. Eventually he was to advocate, and, unbelievably, actually carry out, the murder of six million European Jews, among them some two million children.

But in 1934 the threat was still a lesser one. To be Jewish in Germany then meant to lose your job or be expelled from school, to be taunted and tormented by former friends and colleagues, to have your property confiscated, to be harried and hounded. The blow was the greater because up until January 30, 1933, when Hitler and the Nazi party were voted into power, the German Jews had been completely integrated into German society. Now, suddenly, they were informed that, after all, they did not belong there, that they had no inherent rights or privileges, and that they were members of an inferior and evil race.

Even though no one could predict the grotesque and dreadful shape of things to come, there were people in Palestine and in the United States who felt that an effort should be made to get as many Jewish children as possible out of Germany as soon as possible. But how could such an exodus be organized? Would the children be prepared to leave their homes and parents? Would their parents let them go? Could funds be raised in time?

The answers to most of these questions were found by a small, plump, gentle Baltimore-born lady named Henrietta Szold, who became the leading figure of Youth Aliyah. As Pied Pipers go, she certainly didn't look the part. She was already seventy-four years old, had never been married, and had rarely been known to raise her voice. A teacher, one might guess, or perhaps someone's maiden aunt. But Henrietta Szold, who had indeed been a high school principal once, was, in fact, a general in command of a tiny but extremely effective army of rescue. Reaching out into scores of German-Jewish homes, she coaxed reluctant parents to part with their children, convinced them that grave danger loomed ahead, procured visas and immigration certificates, and created special children's villages in Palestine to which the German youngsters could come. She was concerned with every detail of their settlement in Palestine. They must be made to feel at home, they must be taught Hebrew, they must learn skills which would permit them to earn a living. But most of all, they must be brought out of Europe.

Along with the children, whole families began to leave Germany. In 1935, nearly 70,000 immigrants entered Palestine. Betrayed by their former homeland, rejected and disowned, the Jews of this fourth Aliyah were not as imbued by the romance of Zionism as the Russian and Polish Jews had been, but their contribution to the Jewish community was enormous. The new arrivals made their homes throughout the country; some of them became kibbutz members; others, putting aside careers as doctors, lawyers, and engineers, established model farms, opened shops, and learned to become plumbers and waiters and truck drivers.

All of a sudden, Jewish Palestine acquired a new, neater, more middle-class look. Cultural activities blossomed. The German Jew who had been an organic chemist in Heidelberg and was now a radio repairman in Tel Aviv still wanted to hear Mozart and Beethoven in the evening, to sip beer and discuss German literature, to talk about the cities he had left and the people he had once known. The German Jews wore leather jackets, properly pressed shorts, and sun helmets. They gardened, hummed German lieder, and learned Hebrew only with difficulty. But most important, they were energetic, skilled, and resourceful.

The Arabs of Palestine, panic-stricken by the new wave of immigration, responded with rebellion. Encouraged by Hitler's emissaries in the Middle East and those of Mussolini's Fascist regime in Italy, they saw themselves overrun, dominated by Western civilization and outsiders in the country they had inhabited for so long. Civil war, long simmering in Palestine, now broke out. The Arabs went on strike for months on end, hoping to paralyze the country's economic life; they attacked Jewish settlements, terrorizing the settlers, killing and pillaging. It became dangerous to travel from one town to another.

Bands of armed Arab brigands, many of them from outside Palestine, roamed the land, ambushed Jewish buses, threw bombs into schools and houses, burnt hundreds and thousands of newly planted trees, cut telephone wires and sabotaged trains. They preyed not only on the Jews but also on the Arab *fellahin,* or peasants. Descending on tranquil Arab villages, they forced the frightened men to join them, plundered their meager possessions, agitated and incited until all of Palestine became a land in turmoil.

An Arab Higher Committee was organized to lead the revolt. Its president was Haj Amin el Husseini, the Grand Mufti of Jerusalem, a middle-aged man with a sly face and a criminal record who had diligently acquired many of Hitler's techniques and who was actively aided and abetted by the Nazis. Endowed with much personal charm and a hypnotic manner, the Mufti succeeded in influencing the bewildered Arab masses, and what is more, managed to scare the British. Palestine, he shrilled repeatedly, would go up in flames. The British would be unable to control the fire. The very soil would be scorched. He declared himself to be Mohammed's representative on earth, and the adoring Arabs of Palestine believed and followed him.

Meanwhile, the surge of Arab violence presented a serious problem to the British. Should they continue, as they had promised, to support the steady development of the Jewish national home which they had actually helped bring into being? The hostility toward them throughout the oil-rich Arab countries and the increasing threat of uprisings in Egypt, Transjordan, and Iraq, all of which were British-mandated territories, made it seem unreasonable to go on with the original plan that had been hazily set forth in the Balfour Declaration.

Against the Arab battle cry—"The Government is with us!"—they had to balance the Jewish demand that immigration into Palestine match the rate of expulsion from German-held Europe. Slowly, the British Government gave in; each year, Jewish rights in Palestine were whittled down a bit more. Settlement was restricted to certain parts of the country, and restrictions placed on the number of Jews admitted. To the demand of Jewish settlers that they be allowed to defend themselves against the Arab terror, the Mandatory Government reluctantly allowed exposed and outlying settlements to store a few arms; more often than not they turned out, when needed, to be unusable.

By the spring of 1936 it appeared that the Mufti's dire prediction had come true. Twenty thousand British troops were now stationed in Palestine. Martial law, with its curfews and emergency regulations, was introduced. Official communiques were issued daily from Government House in Jerusalem, making public the news of the continuing murder of Jews. "The High Commissioner regrets to announce . . ." they began. In none of them, however, was the Arab Higher Committee named as the aggressor, nor were the Arab bands charged with being responsible. Some sort of effective self-defense organization clearly had to be created at once. The *Haganah* (the Hebrew word means "self-defense") was the reply of the Jewish community to the lawlessness which no one else, apparently, was going to put down.

The Haganah was an unusual military organization. Made up largely of members of kibbutzim and small villages, it was pledged to defense only, and at no time, despite great provocation, did it depart from its self-imposed discipline. In order to train and arm its people adequately, it was forced to go underground, and although the British knew of its existence, it functioned as a secret organization.

By 1937, most of the able-bodied Jewish population of Palestine was, in some way, linked with the Haganah. In Tel Aviv, which was by now virtually a self-governing city, and which was entirely Jewish, most children above the age of fifteen were sworn into the ranks of the Haganah and worked as couriers, running vital errands on their bicycles and learning to handle weapons. No one ever referred to the Haganah openly; passwords and pseudonyms were in constant use. Even the most spectacular supporter of the Haganah in those days was known throughout the length and breadth of Palestine only as "Hayedid," the friend.

"The Friend" was Captain Orde Wingate, a young, red-haired, short-tempered British intelligence officer who, oddly enough, was a distant relative of T. E. Lawrence, the Englishman who had led the Arab revolt against the Turks in World War I. The son of a Scotch family, Wingate had been reared on the Old Testament, and he had come to Palestine filled with the vision of a great alliance between the British and the Jews. To him, the creation of a Jewish National

Home was the fulfillment of a sacred Biblical prophecy, and he was appalled by British weakness in the face of the Arab guerilla warfare. He made contact with the leaders of the Jewish community. At first they were very suspicious of this strange, ardent, unconventional young man in a British uniform, but in time Wingate convinced them of his sincerity. He declared that all he wanted to do was to help them. The Jews asked him what he knew about Zionism. Wingate's answer was curt: "There is only one important book on the subject—the Bible, and I have read it thoroughly."

He did make a specific recommendation. The Arabs must be fought on their own ground; the Haganah, its principles notwithstanding, must take the offensive. Wingate received permission from the Mandatory Government to train special night squads. He chose one of the kibbutzim as his headquarters, and there he trained and drilled selected Haganah volunteers. He based his teaching on three main concepts, which were, later, to stand the Haganah in great good stead; they were surprise, concentration, and secrecy.

At first, he gave commands and taught in English. No one knew that he spoke any Hebrew. One of the Haganah men training under him tells the story of how they learned that Wingate had mastered the language of the Bible. "We were on our first patrol, creeping forward in the darkness, to unfamiliar Arab terrain. After we had been moving for some hours, Orde halted us. We crouched on the ground, our hearts thudding into our mouths. No one spoke, we hardly breathed. Suddenly, after a long silence, a voice came out of the darkness to us, a voice speaking Hebrew. 'You are the sons of the Macabbees. Why should *you* fear the Arabs?' The exhilaration of that moment, Orde's warm voice coming to us suddenly out of the night, the Hebrew words, the famous historic allusion . . . they all created an impression which none of us ever forgot. After that night, we were never afraid again."

Later that night, as Wingate and his men sat around a

bonfire drinking coffee, he said to them dramatically; "Listen carefully to what I am going to say to you. Today is a memorable day for the people of Israel. Today, you have seen the beginning of the Jewish Army."

Wingate was awarded a British medal for his part in quelling the Arab riots, but he had gone too far. In London, he was made to sign a document stipulating that he would never set foot in Palestine again. In World War II, he became a general and led the victorious Allied campaign against the Italians in Ethiopia. In the end, he was killed in the jungles of Burma, where he had achieved international fame as the leader of the guerilla war against the Japanese.

But all that was still far in the future. For the present, there was Palestine—and the urgent need for the Jews to defend themselves. The Haganah did more than just train men. It began to equip itself. Weapons were bought, stolen, smuggled, even manufactured. All over Palestine, small amateur arsenals sprouted, and cellars and warehouses turned into armories.

The situation was obviously untenable. The British hemmed and hawed, but nonetheless became increasingly alarmed. Finally they decided to send a commission of inquiry to Palestine. It would, they hoped, come up with some workable suggestion for restoring the peace without unduly upsetting the Arabs, who had already declared a widespread boycott of British goods and threatened much worse.

The commission finished its work in 1937. Recognizing the national aspirations of the Jews, responding understandingly to Arab fears of being overrun, it offered a solution—Palestine should be partitioned into a Jewish state and an Arab state. The Jews tended to support the idea, although the projected Jewish state would be a midget entity with a permanent population of half a million. The British were to keep control of all the major cities except Tel Aviv, and actually neither the Jews nor the Arabs would have more than token independence. But at least it would be possible to give shelter to the Jews of Europe, whose situation was becoming more desperate each month. Hitler, unopposed, had gone from destroying synagogues and burning books written by Jews, to imprisoning Jews in concentration camps from which few ever returned whole in mind or body.

The Arabs, however, rejected the idea of partition outright. They were in no mood for compromise. The idea of the twin states died at birth, but the riots did not end. Although most normal functions of civic life had come to a stop, the Jewish drive to reclaim the land continued. The urge to pioneer could not be stopped by bullets.

New settlements defiantly went up on land the Jewish National Fund had bought all over Palestine. Truckloads of young people, guarded by a few Haganah men, traveled at night to the spot selected for settlement; all of the preparations were made very quietly, so that neither the Arabs nor the British would be alerted. Convoys of trucks were made ready—one carrying cans of water and food, another transporting a prefabricated watchtower, a third loaded with parts of a stockade to be nailed together later. As much as possible was done beforehand. Then, at last, the command was given, usually before dawn. The caravan moved ahead slowly through the night. Once at the site of the settlement-to-be, the trucks formed a square, much like the covered wagons of the pioneers in the old West.

As dawn broke, the camp was raised. First the stockade (usually made by pouring crushed rock between wooden frames, over which barbed wire was then draped); then the tall watchtower with its one strong searchlight; and then at last the tents. By mid-morning the new colony was established, given a name, and its members already at work breaking ground for fields and taking turns standing guard.

Between 1936 and 1939, over fifty such settlements were founded overnight in this way, most of them in lonely outposts of the small land.

CHAPTER SIX

Against the Nazi Terror

Leaf through the headlines of the English-language daily newspaper, *The Palestine Post*, published in Jerusalem, for 1937, 1938, 1939, and you have the story of the small but intense, one-sided war which raged virtually unchecked through the Holy Land in those years. Pick a day, any day, and the local news is much the same: crops smoulder in the burned fields of a Jewish farm; bullet holes pierce the side of the Jewish bus which runs from one of the suburbs of Jerusalem into the center of town—the driver and two of the passengers are seriously wounded; a police post in Bethlehem is abandoned by its occupants as indefensible; a new High Commissioner arrives from England and with him come reinforcements of British troops. Now and then, some measure of control is reestablished temporarily, but the underlying tension is never eased.

The Jews and the Arabs filed endless protests with the Mandatory Government. Each side charged the British with discrimination, with wantonly breaking promises, with giving way. The Arabs were more determined than ever to terrorize the country, and the Jews found it harder to abide by their resolution not to retaliate. In the spring of 1939, the Jews and the Arabs were summoned to London for high-level talks with British Colonial officials, but they met at different times and sat around separate tables. Neither side was prepared to concede any major points. The Arabs insisted that all Jewish development in Palestine halt—forever. The Jews, for their part, refused to accept any plan which involved the closing of Palestine's doors to the anguished, desperate refugees. The parallel conferences broke up; nothing at all was accomplished.

On May 17, 1939, the British Government issued a White Paper. The Jews of Palestine read its contents that morning, at first with disbelief, and then with horror. Officially entitled "Command 6019," in effect it confirmed that British support of the Jewish national home had ended. In one dry paragraph after another, the formal decision was spelled out. Jewish immigration into Palestine was to be curtailed at once. Only 75,000 Jews would be allowed to settle there within the next five years. After 1945, the Arabs and the British themselves would decide whether any more Jews would be let in at all. Along with this, the Jewish community was also informed that the further sale of land to them would be drastically limited. Actually, it would be permitted only within an area of less than 300 square miles.

It seemed impossible that the dream which had been so close to fulfillment in November of 1917 had evaporated by May of 1939. But the major concern of the Jews on that hot, depressing May morning was not their own future, nor even the blasting of their high hopes. The fearful questions being asked in every Jewish household in Tel Aviv, Jerusalem, Haifa, and a hundred Jewish rural settlements and colonies throughout the country, were not about themselves. What would happen to the Jews of Europe now? Did no one at all in the British Government understand the extent of their danger? What would become of the wretched, weary queues of terrified men, women, and children who lined up in the waiting-rooms of consulates throughout Europe, pleading for immigration certificates to Palestine? How was it really possible that, in the twentieth century, they could be denied a chance to survive? Could it be, after all, that commercial considerations such as the availability of oil from Arab lands or the threats of boycott by Arab agitators, many of them openly in the employ of Germany and Italy, out-weighed the value of human life?

For the sake of these refugees, who were welcome in no other country in the world, the White Paper could not be accepted. Throughout Palestine, demonstrations and hunger strikes broke out. The Jews announced that they would pay no taxes, that they would recognise not a single one of the new restrictions, and that they would continue their efforts to save the Jews of Europe, White Paper or not.

The Haganah, still adhering, though with growing diffi-culty, to its principle of *Havlagah* (Hebrew for "restraint"), began to beg, borrow, and buy a variety of tiny, dilapidated boats so old and unseaworthy that no one else was prepared to use them, and Haganah emissaries set off for Europe to organize the beginnings of an underground network to rescue refugees and bring them to Palestine. It was a shoddy little armada that was being assembled—but it was unlike any other, and one day it would sail into history. Running the British blockade of Palestine waters became another Aliyah, known tersely as Aliyah Bet, or Ascent II. Later, it would take on more serious proportions and eventually defy the entire British navy, but in 1939 and 1940, blockade-running was still largely a matter of sabotaging British naval and police vessels which patrolled the shores, and of maintaining complicated, expensive contacts in dim offices in the centers of neutral countries such as Turkey and Switzerland and in small Greek and Danubian ports.

Throughout the world, Jews made last-minute attempts to persuade the British to change their minds. The answer was always the same. Everything was being exaggerated, said Britain's harassed leaders. Press reports of the wholesale de-portation, imprisonment, and torture of Jews were clearly being blown up by the Zionists for political reasons. It was absurd to describe Hitler as a latter-day Genghis Khan. In any case, a conference would soon be held to try to solve the problem of the Jewish refugees. As for the White Paper, it would absolutely not be amended.

On September 3, 1939, only a few months after the issuance of the White Paper, the hands of the clock pointed to zero hour. That day, World War II broke out. Hitler, unchallenged, brutally attacked Poland; the Allies, first Britain and then France, declared war on Germany. The Western world was well and truly afire, and a curtain of flame dropped over Nazi-held Europe.

In defeated Poland, whose Jewish population numbered over three million, no hope remained at all. The Jews were herded into concentration camps, locked into ghettos, and dragged into death camps. If life had been close to unendurable for the Jews of Europe before, now they were doomed. A new vocabulary of brutality came into being: Poland was to be *Judenrein,* cleansed of its Jews. Although no statement had yet been made by the Nazis about their final solution of the Jewish problem—the extermination of the Jewish people—it was already clear that the Jewish populations of all the countries threatened by the blustering, victorious Nazis would suffer the fate of Polish Jewry.

There was hardly a family in Jewish Palestine without relatives in Europe. It was as though the rest of the world had closed its ears to the terrified sobs of children, to the unspeakable fears of mothers, and to the torments of those who were trapped in the grip of the Nazis. There was only one decision the Jews of Palestine, sick with anxiety, could possibly make—and they made it at once.

"We shall fight the war as though there were no White Paper," thundered David Ben-Gurion, now chairman of the Jewish Agency and, as such, leader of the Jewish community. "And," he added, "we shall fight the White Paper as if there were no war."

Jews rushed to enlist in the British armed forces. As soldiers they could at least do something concrete to help their imperiled brethren. No less than 136,000 young people registered as potential recruits for a Jewish brigade to fight against the Nazis under its own blue and white flag. But the British had been a world power for a long time and had accumulated considerable political experience. They were not unaware of the fact that if they gave the Jews of Palestine a chance to fight under their own colors, to contribute collectively to the defeat of the Nazis, they would probably demand changes in the White Paper when the war ended. Not unexpectedly, the offer was turned down. No, said the British Government, we really don't need you—yet.

The Jewish Agency for Palestine set up hundreds of recruiting booths in all the major towns. The demand for a Jewish army went on unabated, but in the meantime the Jews of Palestine clamored to fight, anywhere and in any uniform. Very well, said the British, but we will only take one Jewish volunteer for every Arab volunteer.

The Arabs were not particularly anxious to fight for the Allies. They owed them no special loyalty. Throughout the Middle East, in Egypt, Syria, Lebanon, and Iraq, Arab leaders were conducting open and noisy flirtations with the Nazis. The Mufti of Jerusalem, who, along with other Arab extremists, had finally been exiled from Palestine, was now directing the Holy War against Zionism from outside the country, first from Iraq and then from Germany itself. In Iraq, a pro-Nazi government took over in a violent, short-lived putsch.

The British curtailment of Jewish enlistment, however, was not based solely on the desire to keep the number of volunteers equal. With some logic, the British hesitated to train and arm more Jews than absolutely necessary. Trials for the illegal possession of arms were going on all the time in Palestine. Why succumb to emotion and deliver rifles and machine guns into the hands of the very people who might some day use them in their struggle against the Mandatory Government?

But urgent war needs had to be met. Food, drugs, and essential equipment had to be obtained for the thousands of Allied soldiers now stationed in Palestine and the surrounding countries. Suddenly, the diligence and the ability of the Jewish community became an asset to the British. Hundreds of small workshops opened to produce textiles, medicines, and munitions. The kibbutzim and farms went on a wartime footing, and food production rose. Jewish engineers built roads, runways, and radio installations throughout the Middle East, and Jewish technicians repaired cannons, ships, and bridges. The *Yishuv* (the Hebrew word for the Jews of Palestine, literally meaning "The Community") was unalterably committed to Allied victory, and it demonstrated this commitment in every way possible.

The first years of the war went badly for the Allies. Europe crumbled before the onslaught of German tanks and was crushed by the hammering of the Luftwaffe. In the Western Desert, the forces of the British Empire were being pushed back by Rommel's army. It was likely that Egypt might fall to the Germans, and then Palestine. Gradually, the British began to accept more and more Jewish recruits in Palestine. In the end, some 30,000 young men and women entered the British armed forces.

Not all of these were merely soldiers. However reluctant the British had been, initially, to call upon Palestinian Jews for aid, the fortunes of war ultimately dictated the extent and manner of Jewish participation in the war. Scheme after scheme had been put forward by the Jewish Agency and turned down by the British, but finally one idea, out of the many, was too tempting to reject.

It began with the feverish search in Tel Aviv for ways and means of rescuing Jews. By 1944, all Europe lay desolate and ravaged beneath the grim shadow of the swastika. No one knew exactly what had befallen the Jews of Europe, but there was reason to think that many might still be saved. As early as 1942, the Jewish Agency had proposed the organization of an elite corps of parachutists who could perhaps be dropped behind the lines in Nazi-occupied territory to establish rescue operations there. There was no guarantee that the plan would work, but, dangerous though it was, it made sense. Perhaps, heartened by the presence of messengers from Palestine, by the sight of people who deeply cared about them, the Jews of Europe, starved, dehumanized, and condemned to death, might rally, and, in rallying, help to overthrow the Germans. Anti-Nazi guerilla units had already been organized in all the Balkan countries, and perhaps contact could be made with these groups.

By now, Europe was sealed off, a vast fortress with no moat. But no fortress is ever wholly impregnable. Many of the Jews of Palestine were immigrants from the Balkans, their mother tongues Rumanian, Yugoslav, Hungarian. They knew the peoples, the countryside, and the folkways intimately, as no Briton did. They could mingle safely with the Balkan people, with little fear of being detected as foreigners, at least for a while. Also, argued the Jewish Agency, they could collect information for the Allies, help to rescue fallen Allied airmen, and take and bring messages. And they could be trusted implicitly.

In 1943, the disastrous military situation throughout the Balkans at last persuaded British Intelligence to agree to train thirty-two Palestinian volunteers as parachutists. All of them were members of kibbutzim, all hand-picked by the Haganah, and two of them were women.

One of these girls was destined to become a national heroine of wartime Palestine. Young, pretty, incorrigibly romantic, Hannah Senesch had been driven by a sense of mission and the need to sacrifice herself ever since she was a child, growing up in a comfortable, well-to-do middle-class home in Budapest, the city where Herzl had been born. Apart from her charm and her youth, Hannah was also a talented writer; in her diaries, which are now preserved in the collective settlement where she eventually made her home, she described what coming to Palestine at the age of eighteen had meant to her. Its very landscape had moved her profoundly.

"In the freshness of the early morning," she wrote, "I understand why Moses received God's command at dawn. In the mountains, the question arises by itself: whom shall I send?" She answered her own question: "Send *me*."

Life on a kibbutz—the long hard working days, and the uneasy sleepless nights of guard duty—would have been enough of a burden for most young people to bear, however dedicated to the cause. But Hannah Senesch wanted to do more. She found it intolerable to busy herself with even the most arduous of routine tasks while the world she had once known blazed in a frightful conflagration. Torn by the knowledge that the kibbutz relied on every available pair of working hands, and by her own overwhelming urge to become part of the hazardous rescue operations, she finally decided to volunteer as a parachutist. In 1944 she jotted down a few lines in her notebook: "I must go back to Hungary. I must go there now to help to organize the aliyah of children, and to try to bring my mother out. I understand how absurd the idea is, but somehow I feel it is possible."

It *was* possible; Hannah was accepted for training. The plan for her mission was a simple one. Five parachutists were to be dropped in Yugoslavia, and Hannah would cross over into Hungary. Like the others, she wore a British military uniform and a vial of poison was tucked in her boot. Whatever happened, even the very worst, they were never to reveal the real purpose of their mission.

Before she left Yugoslav soil Hannah pressed a piece of crumpled paper into the hands of one of her comrades, On it, she had scribbled four lines:

Blessed is the match that is consumed in igniting the flame.
Blessed is the flame that burns in the secret fastness of the heart.

Blessed is the heart with strength to stop its beating, for honor's sake. Blessed is the match that is consumed in igniting the flame.

She seemed to have known intuitively that she would never survive the mission, and she was right. Almost at once, she was caught and imprisoned. The Germans, who had by now overrun Hungary, treated her with some respect, but the Hungarians were determined to make her speak. They found her mother and brought the two of them together in a dark, narrow prison cell. Unless Hannah told the truth about the nature of her special task, her interrogators told her, not only she, but her beloved mother, too, would die.

During the five months of Hannah's imprisonment, mother and daughter met often. They had been separated for five years and there was much to whisper about. But Hannah's mother never broke under the agonizing strain, even when Hannah was tortured, and Hannah herself seemed made of steel. Once her mother asked her tentatively: "Is it really worth risking your life for an ideal?" Understanding that Mrs. Senesch had guessed that her mission was connected with the rescue of European Jews, Hannah answered simply, "It is, for me."

In the end, she was shot, while her stricken mother stood in the courtyard below. The Hungarians asked Hannah if she wished to plead for mercy. "I ask nothing from hangmen," she said, and faced a firing squad with open eyes.

Much later, other hands reached out to rescue Mrs. Senesch and brought her to Palestine, and Hannah's impassioned poems became part of the literature of the Zionist movement. But she was not the only martyr among the parachutists. There was Enzo Sereni, too. Perhaps, of all the thirty-two, he was the most colorful. He had come to Palestine from Italy, where his father had been personal physician to the king, and he had settled in a kibbutz. Dropped over Italy in May, 1944, he was captured and executed in the infamous Nazi concentration camp at Dachau. He was one of the seven parachutists who did not come back.

There were other, not less spectacular, uses during the war for the young men and women whom the Haganah had surreptitiously trained. When France fell to the Germans in 1941, and the Nazi-supported Vichy Government took over in Syria and Lebanon, it became essential to stop the Nazis from creating outposts in the Middle East. Under British command, the Haganah sent volunteers into Syria to demolish bridges, chart maps, and search out military installations. One of these young men was badly wounded and lost an eye; his name—Moshe Dayan. Years later, he was to become Israel's best-known general.

It was typical of the ironic pattern developing in wartime Palestine, and entirely true to the spirit of Ben-Gurion's paradoxical statement about the White Paper, that only a few months earlier it was the British themselves who had jailed Dayan for illegal possession of arms. He and forty-two others were serving their prison sentences when they were "borrowed" for the Syrian action.

Throughout the war, the Jewish community of Palestine continued to press for the formation of independent and identifiable combat units. But it was only in the final stages of World War II that the British agreed to the creation of the Jewish Brigade. By then, Jewish units, though technically non-belligerent since they were made up not of British subjects but of nationals of a mandatory government, had fought as "Palestinians" in Ethiopia, Iraq, France, Greece, and Crete. At first, they had only been used in transport and maintenance, but later they were allowed to fight.

That a Jewish Brigade was ever formed at all was due largely to ceaseless pressure. Most of it came from Palestine, but some of it from world leaders such as Winston Churchill, to whose imagination and sense of the fitness of things the idea greatly appealed. At last, 5,000 Palestinian Jews, organized in a Brigade Group, and serving under the Zionist colors, met the Nazis in battle, in Italy. The Brigade's value was mainly symbolic, but in an era when millions of Jews, men, women, and children alike, were being brutally put to death, burnt in the massive incinerators and choked in the gas chambers of Nazi death camps, it dramatically expressed the unalterable determination of the Jews of Palestine to play an active part as Jews in the struggle against the most implacable enemy their people had ever encountered.

CHAPTER SEVEN

HAVEN – AT ANY PRICE

THE date: November 27, 1945. The place: the beach at Nahariya, a small resort town in northern Palestine. The time: dawn.

A British coastguard cutter, chuffing vigilantly along the coast, sights a small boat in the rays of the rising sun. On closer examination, it turns out that the boat is lying on her side, some 75 feet from land, and that she is absolutely empty. On the sand near her are strewn a variety of objects—a few boxes, a tin can which once held fresh water, some twine, a child's jacket, a pair of large, torn boots. On her side, someone has placed a Zionist flag, which, somehow or other, the waves that now beat against the boat have not yet managed to displace. Her name is the S.S. *Hannah Senesch*. She is not the first, nor the last, nor even the most famous of the sixty-four odd, leaky, rusty ships which miraculously transported a total of more than 100,000 illegal immigrants from Europe to Palestine in the course of fourteen stormy years. But she is typical of all the others, and so is the story of her human cargo.

World War II came to an end in Europe in August of 1945, and the unspeakable evidence of Nazi crime unfolded before the disbelieving gaze of mankind. The facts were so

.monstrous that, to some extent, they were impossible to digest. Nonetheless, they were true; six million Jews had been murdered. Six million people, guilty only of the fact that they were Jewish, had been done away with. Hitler's ghastly "final solution" had almost worked. Men of goodwill throughout the world recoiled in horror, and Allied troops, sweeping through what had been Nazi-occupied territory, could hardly credit what they saw when they reached the death camps themselves.

Row upon row of walking corpses awaited deliverance. Men, women, and children, so emaciated that they could barely move, crushed in hysterical joy against the barbed-wire fences of the camps, moaned a dreadful welcome to their liberators. Having hung on through years of suffering such as no group of people had ever experienced before, many of them now collapsed, and often literally died of joy. The chaos and the misery were indescribable. Relief organizations rushed into action, producing food, clothing, blankets, and medical care. Vast sums of money were raised and donated to rehabilitate the pitiful survivors—of whom there were estimated to be some one and a half million. Their condition was deplorable; not only were they for the most part physically disabled, but their spirit had been broken. The world had deserted them in the time of their agony, and they trusted no one. They wondered morbidly why they, out of all the millions, had been spared.

There was only one thing they deeply craved, in addition to nourishment and the surcease of pain—to be taken away from the camps in which they had suffered so terribly, to be allowed to live out their days in peace and quiet. But where were they to go? Some tried to return to what had been their homes, and found them either destroyed or occupied. Everything had changed in Europe during the war, and the Jewish survivors belonged nowhere. No one wanted them. They were human leftovers of an unequalled catastrophe, unpleasant reminders of a tragedy that might have been averted, and in no respect at all were they desirable.

But in Palestine, the Jews yearned for them. There, and only there, people were willing to break the law, to steal, to forge, to risk imprisonment and death in order to bring them home, to the Jewish national home for which a frightful justification, never envisioned in 1917, had come into being. In the face of everything that was known now about the plight of the Jews of Europe, it seemed impossible that the White Paper would not be amended. The President of the United States, Harry S. Truman, wrote at once to the British Prime Minister, asking him to allow the immediate admission into Palestine of 100,000 Jewish refugees. The request was rejected. The British refused to change their minds.

The Jews of Palestine now took the law fully into their own hands. Boatloads of survivors, like those who had come to Palestine aboard the S.S. *Hannah Senesch*, were the answer to the adamant stand of the Mandatory Government. The *Hannah Senesch* had been bought, provisioned, and renamed under the auspices of an office created by the Haganah for the specific purpose of the rescue operations. It was called *Ha-Mossad*—"The Institution"—and was responsible for the transport of refugees from various collection centers throughout Europe to the little ports of embarkation where the so-called hell-ships took off for Palestine; also, it was charged with organizing the sea journeys, down to their last details, and, finally, with the landings.

Many of the refugees who traveled on the *Hannah Senesch*, and the other boats like her, had struggled, often on foot, across Europe to the collection centers, staying overnight at special stations where they were fed and housed until the tramp steamers picked them up. Aboard each one of the old, disused freighters that made up the Haganah's small fleet were volunteers from Palestine. The crews were sailors engaged by agents of the Haganah, and their captains were old sea salts from Greece, Crete, Italy, and France to whom the cause of the refugees and the adventure involved in the blockade-running were frequently as attractive as the fees they received for the hazardous clandestine voyages.

The technical problems were staggering. Even the question of getting sailing permits for the derelict boats was complicated. A small Central American republic was the only country willing to run the risk of accepting their registration, and all the Haganah vessels now arrived in Palestine flying a Panamanian flag.

The *Hannah Senesch,* typically, had arrived in the dead of night, dark storm waves dashing against her sides. The crew was alarmed. The landing would be impossible in this weather, they said, speaking from their years of experience on the Mediterranean. It had been a miserable voyage for the several hundred refugees—jammed for days in a fetid hold, eating the minimum of food, and coming up on deck only at night to avoid identification by British patrols. And now the rough seas added a new affliction—everyone was seasick. And even when they landed—and they might not succeed in landing—the refugees knew that danger still lay ahead. If the British caught the ship, and they had caught many, all of her passengers would be imprisoned.

During the war, the British had detained illegal refugees in Palestine itself, letting them out of detention after a while. But now a new war had started, a war against the refugees, and the British were in deadly earnest. However unpleasant it was for young British sailors and soldiers, arms were being used against the refugees, and they were dragged off, caged aboard British destroyers, to imprisonment on Cyprus— behind barbed wire again.

There was no one aboard the *Hannah Senesch* who did not know what had happened to some of the other earlier ships. There was the *Patria,* in 1940, to which 1,900 refugees, having reached haven aboard two captured Haganah vessels, had been forcibly transferred by the British Navy in Haifa. Loudspeakers had informed everyone that the refugees would be taken to exile on an island in the Indian Ocean, and that they would never be permitted to enter Palestine, even when the war ended. The Haganah tried to stop the *Patria* from leaving for her awful destination. Explosives were secretly placed on board in the hope of damaging her engines. But something went wrong, and the *Patria* sank in Haifa bay; 257 refugees, who had managed to escape the death camps, went down with her in full sight of the haven they sought. The British High Commissioner ordered the deportation to go on, nonetheless; but the storm of protest was too much and the double-survivors were allowed to stay in Palestine after all—their number, however, deducted from the quota of available immigration certificates.

Then there had been the *Struma*, a miserable cattle boat, which had left a Black Sea port in 1941 with nearly 800 Jews, including a large number of children. She had put in at Istanbul, because she was so old and overcrowded she was in danger of sinking. The British demanded that the Turkish Government refuse her permission to land and that she be driven away from port. After weeks of discussion and negotiation, the Turks gave in to British pressure. The *Struma* and her hundreds of exhausted, parched, half-starved Jews, without adequate water or food, was chased away. Behind her passengers lay Europe and the Nazis; before them, a chance to endure, at least for the children. Not far from the Straits of Bosporus, she exploded. All aboard, with the exception of one, were drowned.

But the refugees on the *Hannah Senesch* had learned a Hebrew phrase from their Haganah commanders: *Ein Brera*—"there is no alternative"—and they had made their choice. The sea gradually calmed, and the passengers began to sing. Quietly they sang songs of resistance and of redemption, songs of the pioneers in that new land whose contours they could just see through the lifting night. The *Hannah Senesch* slowed down, and hit a sandbar. Nothing could move her; she shuddered deeply once or twice and fell on her side.

Lifeboats were lowered, but the sea turned choppy again, and they were tossed about by the waves. There seemed no way to get to shore. Then someone had an idea. On the shore a group of young Haganah men and women had been waiting for the refugees. They waded into the sea and a rope was passed from hand to hand, creating a living link between the *Hannah Senesch* and the people who had come to welcome her. The youngest and the oldest, the sickest and the most badly crippled of the refugees, were carried ashore, their rescuers holding tight to the wet, rough guideline. From one to another, from one hand to the second, the human chain made its way to land in the pitch dark of a winter night.

The captain of the *Hannah Senesch* was an Italian. He and the crew had made heroic efforts to help everyone land, and now the Haganah feted them. A small secret reception was held somewhere in Palestine a few days later. The captain rose to speak. He lifted a glass and, tears streaming down his cheeks, he said: "We thank you. We hope that we shall return to you many times. Not in small battered boats but in great vessels filled with immigrants." He used the Hebrew word for those who overcome enormous obstacles—*ma'apilim.* It was a new word for illegal immigrants.

An ode was penned to the captain, and although at first it was banned by the British censors, everyone in Palestine soon knew it. In part, it went:

This frail secret fleet, silent and grey will be
The subject of many a song and story,
And many a captain who hears this tale
Will envy you, Captain, your glory.

You'll remember past feats and say to your friends:
I've seen much, but by Santa Maria,
I'll never forget the night of the hunt
As we sped on towards Nahariya.

The immigration continued. So did the British efforts to outwit the Haganah. Ship after ship brought Jews to Palestine —the S.S. *Enzo Sereni,* the S.S. *Henrietta Szold,* the S.S. *Orde Wingate,* the S.S. *Theodor Herzl.* The Haganah issued "passports" for the stateless, displaced persons it brought into Palestine. They read:

Mr. _____ has been found suitable by the Jewish Community of Palestine for repatriation to the Holy Land. Its authority:

1. Ezekiel, 37: "And they shall abide in the land I have given Jacob my servant . . . and they shall abide therein, even they and their children and their children's children forever more."
2. Isaiah, 54: "With great mercies shall I gather thee."
3. The Balfour Declaration, issued on November 2, 1917.
4. The League of Nations Mandate for Palestine.

At a Zionist Congress in London in 1900, Herzl had said, "England, great England, free England, looking over all the seas, will understand our aspirations." Whether the British understood or not, they were now resolute about putting down the open defiance of the Haganah. A law had been passed, and it must be upheld. Besides, the Zionists themselves were to blame for the gruesome conditions aboard the ships of the ma'apilim. Surely it was small mercy to bring Jews to Palestine under such circumstances. If the Haganah were really concerned, above all else, with the welfare of the survivors, it would have tried to persuade them to stay in Europe, to adjust, to forget.

Britain mobilized the full might of her Imperial Navy. Special radar stations were set up to detect incoming Haganah vessels. British destroyers raced back and forth, trying to catch the antiquated refugee boats. The Royal Air Force flew tirelessly on reconnaissance missions, searching for illegal immigrants.

Palestine erupted again. Dissident groups that were not

satisfied with the Haganah's policy of non-retaliation terrorized the British, and the British were quick to respond. Then, in 1947, a ramshackle thirty-year-old American coastal pleasure boat, called the *President Warfield,* whose youth had been spent going up and down Chesapeake Bay, became the spark which was finally to make Palestine too hot, even for the patient British.

The *President Warfield* had had a long and checkered career. During the war, she had briefly ferried Allied troops across the Channel. By 1945 she was on her way to the junk yard, but her engines were still good, she was large, and she was quite capable of making speed. Someone in Baltimore spotted her, paid a lot of money for her, and received her on behalf of the Haganah.

The *President Warfield* sailed from American waters in February, 1947. According to her papers, she was on her way to the Far East, but the Haganah and the British knew otherwise. The British kept an eye on her all the way. They noted exactly when and where she halted for provisioning, tried to persuade the government of Honduras not to register her, and closely watched the new crew that boarded her. The captain was American, as were most of the crew—young Jews, born to freedom and shattered by what they had read about the European holocaust, and eager to help the refugees in any way possible.

From the start of her long voyage, the ship was dogged. British secret-service-men, the Royal Navy, and the RAF followed her wherever she went. In July she reached Sète, a minuscule French port on the Mediterranean, where hundreds of refugees boarded her—1,600 men, 1,282 women, and nearly two thousand children. A huge banner spread amidships now declared that she had been renamed the S.S. *Exodus 1947.*

After weeks of waiting for French permission to sail, the *Exodus* finally left Sète, her passengers unbearably crowded, many of them already ill. A woman died in childbirth. The sanitation system of the ship went to pieces. Her captain drove her as hard as a ship has ever been driven, worried that her boilers would give way. But the *Exodus* held out.

On July 18, at 2:30 A.M., when she was only twenty-two miles from the shores of Palestine, a British destroyer drew up alongside and informed her that she was now in territorial waters and must heave to at once. The *Exodus'* reply was prompt: "On the decks of this ship," said her young commander, "there are over 4,500 people. We will bring them into Palestine as of right, not sufferance. We hold no grudge against your officers and sailors. But we are sorry that they are the instruments of a policy with which we shall never cooperate. The people on this ship are unarmed. We trust you to treat them humanely."

Later, on that still, hot, moonless night, a voice broadcast to Palestine. It was the voice of a Christian clergyman aboard the ship. He told the story of the attack on the *Exodus*. Surrounded by five British destroyers and a cruiser, she was boarded by British troops. "On the deck now there are one dead, five dying, and 120 wounded. We resisted for three hours. Now we must sail for Haifa if we are to save the refugees on board from drowning."

The young clergyman was the Reverend John Grauel of Worcester, Massachusetts. He had offered his services to the Haganah in New York, in any capacity at all, and aboard the *Exodus* he doubled as cook and able-bodied seaman.

Later that day he told the story of the voyage and the boarding: "It was like the Ark, taking these refugees from the waters of death. More than 400 of the women were pregnant. . . . On the night before we expected to land . . . we placed barbed wire over the ship; sent the women and children below; and had almost completed a wooden barricade all around the ship to prevent a boarding party. We estimated we were well beyond the three-mile international limit. If the British attacked us now, they would be guilty of piracy.

"But," Mr. Grauel went on, "that's precisely what hap-pened. . . . Two British ships suddenly reappeared. Their searchlights bathed us in a light as bright as noon. They took their positions, one on either side of us; they were going to ram us!

"I pulled the ship's whistle, to give the alarm. We lined up every able-bodied man on the deck, each of us armed with potatoes, wood, tinned goods: and in that bright light from the cruisers, with the flag of Zion blowing, and the high, shrill whistle shrieking, we waited for the blow.

"Then they struck us. They rammed us hard—slow, power-ful, and terrible. . . . We were thrown to our knees. They rammed us again and again—seven times in all. We clung to each other, to whatever we could grasp, thinking of the panic of those poor souls below decks, jammed together so they could hardly breathe; and in the midst of it, waiting for the next blow, an old Jew muttered beside me: 'I have already survived in my life the Czarist Russian hell, the Polish anti-Semitic hell, the Nazi hell, and so help me God, I shall survive this too!'

"We were rammed the seventh time; and then British sailors, carrying clubs, pistols, and tear-gas grenades, boarded us. At one corner they were halted by children: the British shot at them. . . .

". . . They dropped drawbridges to the deck of our ship and charged across. Our boys took four of them prisoner and I had the four placed in my cabin and put two of our men on guard at the door. I knew our people were very angry and might harm them.

"Then, one of our boys ran to me and said the British had gained control of the bridge and a seriously wounded man was in the captain's cabin. I wrapped an American flag on my arm and ran to the bridge. A British sailor was there. 'We've got a wounded man in there,' I said. 'I beg you let me go in and get him.' But the sailor refused to let me see him, and I had to retreat. When the British reached the bridge, they had thrown open the door and fired, without any warning."

The Reverend Grauel paused to catch his breath. He had not slept for sixty hours. Then he continued.

"Finally, we negotiated with the British. The fighting was stopped and one of the ship's officers—an American—took the wheel and we went into Haifa port. There was no need for the boarding party to have used bullets. The refugees aboard the *Exodus* were unarmed. We had made a thorough search two days earlier and found three pistols. I myself saw them thrown overboard. All the immigrants had to fight with were potatoes, canned goods, and their bare fists. But it was all no use. They will come to Palestine. I know these people; nothing short of open warfare and complete destruction will stop them."

That morning, all the schools and shops in Palestine closed in a silent sympathy strike. The sick and wounded on the *Exodus* were taken to hospitals, while all of the other passengers were dragged into giant cages set up on the decks of three British transport ships waiting for them in the harbor. Then, the British announced their decision. They would return the refugees to Europe. The *Exodus*, they proclaimed, was to serve as an example.

The world was shaken; cables and telephone calls from the four corners of the earth attempted in vain to intercede on behalf of the refugees. Prayers were offered in churches and synagogues everywhere. The British soldiers guarding the three prison ships were visibly repelled by their task, but at the scheduled time the three ships sailed inexorably westward.

They arrived in France, at Port de Bouc, near Marseilles. The refugees, all hope gone, prepared for passive resistance. Nothing worse could happen than that they be sent back to the lands of their purgatory and bereavement. The British disclaimed all responsibility for the suffocated masses aboard the ships, and put heavy pressure on the French to give them no help, except for food and water. The French said they would not force anyone off the ships but offered asylum to any refugee who chose to land. But the refugees had decided; not a single one would leave. For scorching weeks they sat inside the wire cages—either they would land in Palestine or not at all.

So the ships set sail again, this time for Germany. There, in Hamburg, in the British-occupied zone of Germany, the Jews were at last disembarked. Those who refused to leave the ships were beaten and forced off, while Germans stood around and watched, pondering the ways of man and history.

The refugees were interned at Lubeck. Most of them were later to make their way again to Palestine, after 1948. The British had won the round, but it marked the beginning of the end of their rule in Palestine, and it left scars which seemed unlikely ever to heal.

CHAPTER EIGHT

THE DIE IS CAST

ONE morning in June, 1947, eleven men descended from a plane that had just touched down at Lydda airport in Palestine. Each one represented a member state of the United Nations—Australia, Canada, Czechoslovakia, Guatamala, Holland, India, Iran, Peru, Sweden, Uruguay, and Yugoslavia. Together with some fifty aides, translators, liaison officers, and typists, they made up the United Nations Special Commission on Palestine, whose name was to be clipped to UNSCOP in the course of the following months.

Their mission was formidable. On behalf of the United Nations, they were to study the situation in Palestine, to listen to and assess the arguments of all concerned parties, and to return to UN headquarters at Lake Success in New York with some kind of workable solution. They had arrived in the Holy Land at a time described by one of the Commission as "a moment touched by history in tragic fashion."

The more extreme elements of the Jewish underground had now openly proclaimed defiance not only of the British, but also of the Haganah itself. Two terrorist organizations had come into being. One, by far the larger, was the *Irgun Zvai Leumi* (the National Military Organization), which believed in swift retribution and in instant retaliation, regardless of the consequences. Within its own ranks, discipline was exemplary, but it refused to take any orders from the Haganah or to be swayed by considerations of diplomacy or reasonableness. The Irgun's motto was *Rak· Kach* ("Only thus") and its emblem a raised hand holding a rifle. Like the Haganah, the Irgun ran its own paper and operated a secret wireless station. But unlike the Haganah, it was dedicated to the proposition that the British must be driven out of Palestine at all cost, and it staged attacks on British installations, government buildings, and eventually on personnel.

The other splinter group, which was much smaller, called itself "Fighters for the Freedom of Israel," but it was known as the Stern Group, after the name of its first leader. The Sternists were relentless; their professed aim was the assassination of their enemies. They were dedicated, dangerous, and enormously skilled at escaping from their pursuers.

The British were now faced by circumstances which even they began to regard as intolerable, and in despair they turned to the United Nations for help. An irresistible force had met an immovable object. No one involved in the struggle would give way to anyone else. After twenty years of rule in Palestine, the British found themselves spending increasing amounts of money and manpower on totally unsuccessful attempts to force the Jews and the Arabs to keep the peace. Let the United Nations cope with the problem now.

The Jewish Agency and the Haganah, which represented the majority of the Jews of Palestine, continued, undaunted, to bring in boatload after boatload of illegal immigrants. The British, equally undaunted, continued to board the ships, arrest the passengers, and haul them off to detention camps in Cyprus.

The Haganah also went on with the job of acquiring arms. An elaborate secret organization, so security-conscious that many of its members did not know of each other's affiliation with it, was set up. Called *Rekhesh* (Hebrew for "Acquisition"), its volunteer agents worked throughout Europe—

under assumed names, with forged papers, often in disguise. Their task was to buy and ship arms, whenever and wherever they could lay their hands on them. Weapons were not hard to find in the aftermath of World War II as long as money was available, but getting them into Palestine was another matter. The country was now blockaded from all sides and bristling with troops. Even the most innocent package was virtually torn apart by jittery customs inspectors to make sure that its stated contents were really harmless. The days when the Haganah could hide arms inside cases of books or personal possessions were over.

Although the methods used for arms smuggling in 1947 were ingenious, they were intricate, time-consuming, and expensive, and the total amount of weapons brought into Palestine was pitifully small. One idea which worked for a while was to dismantle the weapons, carefully marking the separate parts so they could be easily reassembled, and hide them inside specially constructed bogus machines, which were then crated and shipped to Palestine as heavy agricultural and industrial equipment. The job was immensely complicated. To begin with, Rekhesh approached several of the largest Jewish companies in Palestine which were licensed to import steamrollers, combines, mechanical looms, and similar machines. These companies agreed to help, not only with licenses, but with shipping space and even with money.

The Haganah set up a series of small workshops throughout Europe, usually in isolated farmhouses or empty villas, and there the fantastic pseudo-machines were built. Inside each one, cavities were made to contain arms, TNT, cordite, and so on. The machines were packed in specially constructed crates and trucked by Rekhesh drivers to the docks. In this and other devious ways a steady trickle of rifles, submachine guns, spare parts, and rounds of ammunition was reaching the Haganah.

But importing weapons was not enough. A miniature arms industry was set up in Palestine itself, in cellars, garages, and abandoned air-raid shelters, and at the same time, the Haganah accelerated its raids on British munition dumps and armories. Sympathetic British Army personnel, moved by the inadequacy of the Haganah's supplies, and by the desire to redress the balance of arms in Palestine, sometimes helped, occasionally for money but often out of goodwill. The Arabs, oddly enough, helped out too, both as highly competent smugglers and as ordinary dealers.

Of course, the more arms the Haganah was able to accumulate, the more thorough became the British searches. Mandatory police and troops turned Palestine inside out, looking for Haganah caches. Raiding parties rumbled into one settlement after another, rounding up men, ransacking houses, and churning up the earth.

Since self-defense was not recognized as grounds for possessing arms, the military courts tried any Jew caught with a revolver and a few rounds of ammunition and handed down stiff sentences. This also accomplished nothing. Palestine's Jews were preparing for major and unavoidable conflict, either with the British or with the Arabs, or with both, and some sort of stockpiling was essential.

The Haganah went out of its way to try to prevent the situation from worsening, but the Irgun and the Stern Gang became increasingly reckless. When the British caught and flogged Irgun members, the Irgun caught and flogged British soldiers. When the British hanged three young Irgunists who, disguised as British soldiers, had taken part in a huge prison break that freed more than a hundred political prisoners, the Irgun kidnapped and executed two British sergeants. It also became involved in large-scale terrorist operations against the British, many of which resulted in the death of Jews, Arabs, and Britons alike. One such was the bombing of a wing of a Jerusalem hotel used as British Army Headquarters. Although the Irgun warned the British to vacate the premises, the warning went unheeded and ninety-five persons died in the terrible explosion.

The British, for their part, tyrannized the entire Jewish community. One day, troops took over the buildings of the Jewish Agency, arrested all its leaders and another two and a half thousand people, and interned everyone for weeks. From time to time, British troops, unbearably provoked, ran amok, firing on peaceful elements of the population, claiming that they were terrorists. The streets of Jerusalem looked as though the Holy City were under siege. The Mandatory administration lived and worked behind barbed wire barriers, in special security zones, constantly surrounded by heavily armed soldiers.

Despite the presence in Palestine of 50,000 British troops, the Arab nationalists continued in a familiar pattern: ambushes, sniping, demolition, and strikes. They also continued to prey on the Arab peasants, extorting money, destroying their property, and threatening to kill them at the first sign of any cooperation with the Jews.

It was in this tense atmosphere that the gentlemen of UNSCOP deplaned. In a carefully guarded convoy of twenty-six cars, they traveled throughout the country, interviewing, observing, asking questions, and taking notes. The Arab nationalist leaders at once declared that they would not appear before UNSCOP in Palestine and kept their word. But UNSCOP had come to find out what was wrong and, despite the non-cooperation of the Arabs, did its job most diligently. It assembled vast files of facts and figures, noted the growing disparities between the aspirations of the 600,000 Jews and of the 1,100,000 Arabs, and listened attentively to many witnesses, among them David Ben-Gurion and the aging Dr. Chaim Weizmann, and even journeyed to Transjordan to talk to King Abdullah.

On the last day of August, 1947, UNSCOP completed its report, which was short, to the point, and very specific. Not unlike the Royal Commission Report of 1936, UNSCOP concluded that the only possible solution to the Palestine problem was partition. It recommended that the country be divided into two separate and sovereign states, one Arab and one Jewish. Each state would contain the largest possible number of its own people. The Jewish state was to be made up of the eastern part of the Galilee, the fertile Valley of Jezreel (also called the Plain of Esdraelon), much of the coastal plain, which of course included Tel Aviv, and part of the Negev. The Arabs were to get Western Galilee, the hill country of central Palestine, Judea, and a strip along the southern coast. As for Jerusalem, that city of man's eternal desire, it was to belong to everyone. UNSCOP recommended that Jerusalem be placed under international control. The land area of the two states was to be more or less the same, although more than half of the Jewish state was to consist of the Negev, which was virtually rainless and where no one lived, except for Bedouin nomads.

There was much to be said for the plan—and much against it. It would allow the Jews to bring in all those who needed or wanted to enter Palestine, and it would, at last, fulfill the dream of a Jewish state. The borders would be hard to defend, but this was no time for haggling. Although many Jews had grave misgivings about the size and dimensions of the projected state, and the fact that it excluded Jerusalem, the plan won their reluctant approval. The Arabs rejected it, sight unseen; they would not accept the authority of the United Nations in this matter, they said, nor would they lend a hand in any way to the creation of a Jewish state. And further, added the spokesmen for the Arab states, they would collectively drive the Jews into the sea. The Jewish state, if born at all, would be crushed before it drew its first breath.

On Saturday, November 29, 1947, the General Assembly of the United Nations met in New York. A two-thirds majority vote was required to implement UNSCOP's proposal. In the hushed hall, one delegate after another rose to register his nation's vote. The roll-call was in alphabetic order, and took a long time. Thousands of miles away, in Palestine, the Jews sat beside their radios. Would enough states affirm the wisdom of UNSCOP's recommendation and bring a Jewish state into being? How would Great Britain vote? And France? And Bolivia?

Weeks of pressure and counter-pressure, of lobbying and explaining, had preceded that historic Saturday afternoon; now, what would the fifty-eight member nations of the UN decide? The tension mounted. The voting droned on. How would Haiti vote? And the Philippines? And the Soviet Union?

"Yes."

"Yes."

"No."

"Abstention."

"Yes."

Finally, the votes were in, and tallied.

The president of the General Assembly rose to announce the result. Thirty-three states had declared themselves in favor of the partition of Palestine, thirteen had gone on record as opposed to it, eleven abstained, and one was absent. The world, in the multi-faceted person of the United Nations, had legally created two new states.

In Palestine, a sigh of relief went up from the Jewish community. After weeks of anxiety, it was done, over with, finished. All that night, the Jews celebrated; they danced and sang and congratulated one another. Here and there, as they jammed the streets, they were joined by patrolling British troops, swept up in the massive enthusiasm of the moment. In the floodlit courtyard of the Jewish Agency building in Jerusalem, a crowd slowly gathered and began to sing the Zionist anthem, *Hatikvah* ("The Hope"). It was almost fifty years to the day that Herzl, coming home after the opening of the first Zionist Congress in Basle, had confided to his diary: "Today, I founded the Jewish State. If I were to say so now, people would laugh at me. But in five years time, certainly in 50 years, it will be seen that I was right." No one was unaware of what loomed ahead; no one was insensitive to the fact that only a few feet away, in the walled Old City, the representatives of the Arabs had gathered for final consultations on their official response. But for the moment, for that one night in November, all was jubilation, happiness of a sort that would never be forgotten by those who experienced it.

In the morning, the Arabs had acted. They called a three-day strike throughout the country, and the first blow fell: two Jewish buses traveling to Jerusalem were attacked and six people were killed, the first victims of partition. By December 2, there were Arab riots all over the country. Tired of the effort, the expense, the futility of trying to keep the peace, the British stopped governing altogether. They kept control, but they made no attempt to intervene in what was already the prelude to war. Palestine hurtled towards chaos. The British withdrew behind their barricades and road blocks, and waited to get out. The UN had made a decision; let the UN enforce it.

But the British White Paper was not abrogated. Illegal immigrants were still not allowed to enter. The British no longer controlled the highways of Palestine, now open to whatever armies might march in, across the frontiers, from Syria, Lebanon, Iraq, Egypt, Transjordan, and Saudi Arabia. But the arms searches went on. So did the retaliatory terrorism of the Irgun and the Stern Group. Irregular forces of the Arab states began to infiltrate Palestine, and the British looked the other way.

On December 6, the British Government announced that the Palestine Mandate would be terminated on May 15, 1948, and the withdrawal of all British troops would be completed by August. In the meantime, the Jews prepared to face two major fronts at once. They readied themselves to govern a state, and to defend it.

The Jewish Agency had used its large measure of autonomy well; for years it had been a kind of shadow government, existing alongside the Mandatory Government. It ran its own department of external affairs, its own department of political affairs, and its own treasury, complete with the machinery of taxation. It controlled its own health services, educational network, and defense establishment. On its councils sat men and women of many different political shadings, from radical socialists to conservative right-wingers. Although bitterly divided about the extent and manner of resistance to the British, the Jewish community, in general, was disciplined, united, and, of course, eager for independence.

But the problems of defense were urgent. The fact was that the Jews had no artillery or anti-aircraft guns, no tanks, no air force, and no naval vessels. The Haganah could call on some 45,000 men and women, of whom only a few thousand were properly trained, plus some 3,000 members of the Irgun and a few hundred members of the Stern Group. Mustering every available weapon, the Jews had a few thousand rifles of different makes, about 3,000 submachine guns (many of which were homemade), about 300 light machine guns, 200 medium machine guns, some two- and three-inch mortars, and less than 20 anti-tank rifles. They also had some locally produced grenades and Molotov cocktails.

The Arabs called for a Holy War from a thousand minarets throughout the world. Their armies, now poised to invade as soon as the British departed, had tanks, artillery, armored cars, aircraft, warships, and as much ammunition as they needed. Even if the Palestinian Arabs had wanted to set up the Arab state proposed by the UN—and there is reason to believe that some did—they were overwhelmed by the incessant and shrill propaganda of the Arab nations pressing for the annihilation of the Jews.

November 29, 1947, marked many milestones; among others, it marked a desperate effort by the Haganah to arm itself before the Mandate ended. The UN decision to partition Palestine had been supported both by the United States and Russia, but no arms were made available by any of the great powers, and an embargo was declared on all arms shipments to the Middle East.

The Haganah scoured Eastern Europe, and turned at last to Czechoslovakia. Czechoslovakia was less than ideal, geographically, for arms running. She was landlocked and all her routes to the open sea involved complicated transit. But the Czechs were big munition makers, and anxious to receive foreign currency. A secret Haganah delegation went to Prague to negotiate. Posing as South Americans, the Haganah mission finally succeeded in buying some 10,000 rifles and about 400 machine guns. But by the time the deal was concluded, the situation in Palestine had become too acute for sea or land transport to be used. Rekhesh organized an airlift, using a plane hastily chartered in the United States.

Other arms had to be sent by sea. A small boat, the S.S. *Nora*, was loaded with potatoes in Venice and sent to a Yugoslav port to pick up the Czech arms. The potatoes were hauled off, the arms were loaded, and the potatoes put back on top of them. The *Nora* made her way to Israel in a violent storm and arrived safely in the harbor of Tel Aviv.

The spring of 1948 was filled with violence. The Arabs attacked endlessly; their guerillas crossed the borders wherever possible. Fighting broke out on the coastal plain, in the Galilee, in the Negev. From north to south, the Haganah deployed to stave off the Arab bands, each one now numbering from seven to eight hundred uniformed men. By April of 1948, 1,200 Jews had been killed.

But the greatest danger was to Jerusalem. Perched high on the hills of Judea, vulnerable from every side, and housing one sixth of the Jewish population, the Holy City was now actually under siege. The only access to the rest of the Jewish population was a winding, forty-mile-long mountain road which was controlled by Arabs. Until it could be freed, no supplies would reach Jerusalem; for weeks, the city lived on iron rations, bread and water being allotted to each resident by a "war cabinet" set up by the Jewish Agency.

But semi-starvation was not the only burden Jerusalemites were to shoulder. The Jewish section of the city held out against ferocious daily bombardment. The British were not much of a deterrent any more; once they left, the Arabs would obviously try to capture this shining prize.

An important military action took place early in the year at Mishmar HaEmek, a kibbutz in the Plain of Esdraelon, southeast of Haifa. In April, a thousand Syrian and Iraqi irregular troops, together with some 500 Palestinian Arabs, pounded the settlement with cannon, tanks, and planes. The settlers sent the women and children away, and counter-attacked, mostly with rifles and hand grenades. The Arab force was routed only after two weeks of fighting. The women and children of the kibbutz came back and work in the fields was resumed. The dead were bitterly mourned, but the victory was a sign and a symbol of things to come. Imagination, surprise, daring—all that Wingate had preached to the Haganah—now began to weigh in favor of the Jews.

Jerusalem, however, was still in mortal peril. In April, David Ben-Gurion, working from Haganah headquarters in Tel Aviv, marshalled a convoy of three hundred vehicles to go into battle for the city's life. It was seventeen miles long, and on the first truck were chalked the words: "If I forget thee, O Jerusalem, let my right hand forget its cunning." The convoy got through, but it was the last to go up to Jerusalem for a long time. The Arabs retained command of the main road, and Jerusalem was now completely isolated.

Other major towns fell to the Haganah, some easily, others after intensive battles. Haifa, Tiberias, Safed, Jaffa—all were in the hands of the Jews before the Mandate ended. Despite the casualty lists, the prisoners, the sounds and smell of battle, it was not yet, formally, a war. Nor was there yet, officially, a Jewish state. But time was running out. On May 15, the British flag would be lowered over Government House, and the Jews and Arabs, however unequally matched, would at last be left alone for their fateful confrontation.

CHAPTER NINE

A STATE IS BORN

IT was 4:30 A.M. on May 14, 1948, when Martha Hunter Black, a middle-aged Protestant missionary from England, woke up in her room at the Mission Hospital Compound in Jerusalem. She had set her alarm for this early hour to be sure of being able to brew a cup of tea before the water was shut off. Jerusalem, cut off from the rest of Palestine by a tight Arab blockade, was on emergency rations of fuel, food, and water. The night before, Miss Black had sat up listening to the High Commissioner for Palestine, Lieutenant General Sir Alan Cunningham, broadcast his farewell message. Immediately afterwards, she made an entry in her diary: "He ended abruptly with 'Good-bye.' It broke over me for the first time that Britain, my country, was leaving the Holy Land."

Miss Black turned to her morning chores. In the Old City, on the other side of town, fruit and vegetables were still to be found. On the way, she passed the British administrative enclave, nicknamed "Bevingrad" in ironic tribute to His Majesty's Foreign Secretary, Ernest Bevin. Inside Bevingrad, harassed British officials and soldiers were busy packing.

Elsewhere in Jerusalem, a Jewish newspaperman, by day a correspondent for a British daily, by night the unnamed

announcer for the secret Haganah radio, "Voice of the De-
fender," leaned out of his window and watched the sun come
up over Mount Scopus and the Mount of Olives. Writing
to his daughter in London, he said, "For the moment, time
hangs suspended. Any minute, it may break into violent
motion. Soon, I shall go up to the roof to see if I can watch
the High Commissioner leave."

He had saved a pair of binoculars from the clutches of
the Haganah, which, by now, had requisitioned everything
that could conceivably be of any military use. With them
he intended to observe what, in his broadcast the night before, he had accurately called the end of an era.

Not far away, a cameraman, working for an international
company, sniffed unhappily at the dawn. He was to be the
only outsider to accompany the High Commissioner on his
exit from Jerusalem, but at the moment he wondered whether
the scoop was worth the danger. His status as representative
of a movie company would hardly help him with the Arabs,
to whom he would simply be a Jew on the loose in the wrong
part of town. He strapped film magazines around his waist,
wishing they were cartridges.

The Arab zone looked half empty. A long ribbon of motor
transport was assembled for the British exodus. The cameraman reached Government House on time, but just as he set
up his equipment, a command echoed across the parade
ground. A solitary bagpiper skirled a Highland lament. The
Union Jack came down and a Red Cross flag was raised in
its place. The High Commissioner, in full dress uniform,
stepped into his Rolls Royce. The motorcade swept down
the pine-lined driveway. The High Commissioner was
scheduled to fly to Haifa, where a cruiser awaited him. The
route to the airport led through Arab quarters, and along
the way, crowds began to gather, mostly in silence, broken
by a few jeers. At 8 A.M., three Spitfires, Sir Alan's escort,
were already airborne. During the flight to Haifa, the High
Commissioner was silent, peering down at the green land-

scape. At one point he asked, of no one in particular: "How can they divide this country?"

At ten past eight, Zipporah Ben-Tovim saw the air escort flying north in perfect formation. Zipporah lived with her husband Arieh, an engineer, and two school-age daughters in a suburb of Jerusalem, on the road to Tel Aviv. For weeks, the Ben-Tovims had spent their nights in a makeshift shelter and had become accustomed to sneaking out of the house under snipers' fire to pick wild grape leaves and various more or less succulent weeds to cook on a small fire in the garden. Arieh spent his nights away on Haganah patrol duty and had not yet returned. He appeared just before nine, with news. Haganah troops, hidden all night in nearby buildings, had watched the British pull out of their enclave and had rushed in, ahead of the Arabs. It was an unexpected victory. Arieh hugged Zipporah and dashed out again, back to headquarters. Zipporah, half wishing that the British had kept their promise to stay until August, sighed and went on washing the floor.

In Haifa, Sir Alan wearily took a salute from a fifty-man company of the Palestine police and shook hands with the Jewish mayor and the Arab vice-mayor. Beyond the harbor, he could see the cruiser *H.M.S. Euryalus.* "Good going-away weather," Sir Alan remarked, and at exactly 9:30 A.M., he boarded the cruiser's launch. A band played "God Save the King," a guard of honor presented arms, and the Union Jack was lowered for the last time.

In Tel Aviv that morning, the Jews were getting ready to take over, under conditions so precarious and unpredictable that their efforts mixed high drama with a certain amount of grim comedy. The punch line of a current joke went: "Two thousand years, we waited for a state—and it had to happen to me!"

The British withdrawal was accompanied by a maximum of confusion. Palestine was left, abruptly, with no airmail or sea mail and seriously lamed internal communications.

Weeks ago the British had stopped collecting taxes, registering cars, maintaining health controls. They had destroyed land deeds and dispersed all government archives. They had frozen Palestinian assets in England and removed most of the local currency.

On the morning of May 14, 1948, the prospective Jewish government lacked everything from proper offices to a constitution, from a civil service to an adequate army. But preparations went full steam ahead. A Council of the People, consisting of representatives of the Jewish population and of the World Zionist Organization, had been formed and was drawing up plans for a provisional government.

That day, four field-guns, vintage 1912, were secretly brought into the country. Other items were on order, but there was no way of knowing when they would arrive. Despite the Haganah's early success in defending the New City of Jerusalem, the situation there was far from certain, while inside the Old City, it seemed all too certain: there, some 1,500 Jews were surrounded by Arabs who outnumbered them at least fifteen to one.

To make matters worse, the Haganah commander-in-chief was ill and his responsibilities had been shifted, at the last minute, to Yigael Yadin, a thirty-year old archaeologist. Yadin was to leave a considerable mark on Israeli military affairs, not only by winning battles, but by creating a modern military vocabulary in Hebrew—a language at home with such weapons as spears, arrows, and asses' jawbones, but hardly with mortars or incendiary bombs. Among the new terms contributed by Yadin was the Hebrew word for brigadier general, his own rank, and the highest in the Israeli army. The main burden of command, however, rested on the square shoulders of sixty-two-year-old David Ben-Gurion, labor leader, politician, farmer, and philosopher.

At about the time that Martha Black had gotten up in Jerusalem that morning, Ben-Gurion had gone to bed in Tel Aviv. With the dozen or so men who formed the Haganah high command, he had spent the night going over plans for coping with the imminent invasion. It had been decided to declare "State D"—extreme emergency—and to order the population to dig trenches and build roadblocks (an activity in which they were to indulge twice again in the next twenty years). The three planes capable of carrying passengers were assigned to evacuate outlying settlements, and Ben-Gurion again made clear his decision, taken in the face of sound professional advice, not to concentrate the scattered Jewish forces but to order them to defend whatever part of Palestinian soil they then held. This was roughly the entire coastal plain from Haifa to Tel Aviv, an area of about twenty miles south and southeast of Tel Aviv, and a network of roads in the southern peninsula.

By 4 A.M., Ben-Gurion was home asleep. Later, he turned to the mound of messages and wires that brought the first of the day's pressing business. The news from the settlements was bad. Kfar Etzion, largest of four Jewish kibbutzim in the hills between Bethlehem and Hebron, had been virtually overrun, and there was no choice but to order its defenders to capitulate. Beit Ha-arava, a small settlement on the Dead Sea, asked that its people be evacuated. A plane had been sent to them, but had broken down en route; could another plane be spared? There was also a report from an emissary of the Jewish Agency who, two nights earlier, disguised in Arab robes, had driven beyond the borders of Palestine to Transjordan, hoping to reach some sort of last-minute agreement with King Abdullah. Over coffee, the King had told his visitor that war could be avoided only if the Jews gave up the idea of establishing a state.

But, for better or for worse, Ben-Gurion was going to proclaim a Jewish state that day. A small group known grandly as "The Committee of the Situation" was in charge of the arrangements. A suburb of Tel Aviv, Sarona, had been selected as the seat of the new government. The offices were sup-

Theodor Herzl stood for this portrait around 1895.

Among Arabs and Europeans, Herzl sits on the deck of a ship bound for Palestine in 1898.

An early portrait of the young French army captain, Alfred Dreyfus, before he was charged with treason.

European settlers camped on the site of Petach Tikvah, the first pioneer village in Palestine, around 1878.

Archives of the State of Israel.

*Above, settlers at Degania,
the first kibbutz,
or collective settlement,
in 1912.*

*Sir Herbert Samuel, first High
Commissioner of Palestine, with
Emir Abdullah on his right and
Winston Churchill on his left.*

Archives of the State of Israel.

*Dr. Chaim Weizmann (on the
left) with Emir Feisal in
Palestine, about 1918.*

The Exodus in an Italian port in April, 1947, shortly before her historic attempt to break the British blockade.

Refugees leaving the Exodus in Haifa port on July 18, 1947. The wreckage marks where a British ship rammed the Exodus.

Tel Aviv residents celebrating the United Nations vote approving an independent state of Israel, on November 29, 1947.

David Ben-Gurion, the first Prime Minister of Israel, reading the Declaration of Independence on May 14, 1948, in Tel Aviv.

*Yemenite Jews on board a
transport plane taking them
to Israel during Operation
Magic Carpet, in May, 1952.*

Israeli soldiers preparing to move into the Gaza Strip during the war with Egypt in 1956.

Below, Israeli troops advance in the western Sinai in November, 1956.

Wide World Photos

The Knesset, Israel's Parliament, situated in Jerusalem.

Adolf Eichmann standing in his bulletproof-glass prisoner's dock, during his trial in Jerusalem in the summer of 1961.

Part of the Old City of Jerusalem, looking toward the Dome of the Rock and the Mount of Olives. The Tower of David is in the front.

*Above, the fortress
Massada by the Dead Sea,
showing the excavations of the
palace of Herod the Great.
Left, Professor Yigael Yadin,
leader of the 1963–1965
archaeological expedition,
at Massada.*

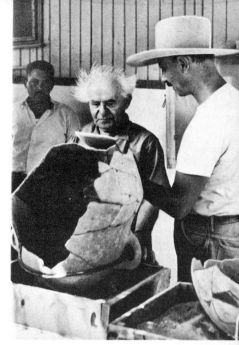

Professor Yadin discussing some artifacts with David Ben-Gurion at the Hebrew University.

Below, part of the lower terrace of Herod's palace at Massada.

*A narrow road meanders
through the vast desolation
of the Negev, Israel's
southern desert.*

Overlooking the Wilderness of Zin in the Negev.

Below, a modern kibbutz in the Negev desert.

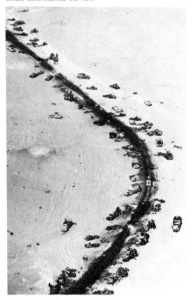

An Egyptian convoy in the Sinai Desert destroyed by an Israeli air attack during the Six Day War of June, 1967.

Below, the Greek Orthodox monastery of St. Catherine, on the slopes of Mt. Sinai in the southern Sinai desert.

*Above and below left: Israeli soldiers at the Wailing Wall
in the Old City of Jerusalem on June 8, 1967, after
taking the Holy City from Jordanian soldiers. Below right:
Israel's Minister of Defense, General Moshe Dayan, holding
some flowers just picked from a crevice in the Wall.*

Israel and her neighbors as seen from a space capsule. Israel is at the upper left, at the eastern end of the Mediterranean Sea. The Sinai Peninsula is in the center, flanked by the Gulfs of Suez and Aqaba. The dark area in the lower left is part of the capsule.

posed to be ready for occupancy, but were not. The text of the actual proclamation of independence still needed ironing out; it also had to be stenciled and distributed to the press. Another problem was that it had to be inscribed on parchment, and a young graphic designer had searched all Tel Aviv for parchment in vain.

Tel Aviv's art museum, a singularly unpretentious and, in fact, somewhat shabby building, had been chosen as the place for the ceremony. The time and place of the proclamation were known at this stage only to the engineers of the secret Jewish radio. Some two-hundred people had been invited to the ceremony, which was due to start at 4 P.M. Ben-Gurion approved the arrangements and a few final suggestions. Flags would be needed, and of course a picture of Theodor Herzl.

In the main Tel Aviv post office, new stamps were being sorted. Designed several weeks earlier, they bore the non-committal inscription *Doar Ivri*—"Hebrew Mail"—since the name of the new state had not yet been decided upon. It was still not decided upon; in the discussions, "Zion" and "Judea" had almost as many supporters as "Israel." Nine denominations of stamps had been printed on a letterpress and transferred at night from the plant of a Hebrew newspaper to an abandoned shed on the outskirts of Tel Aviv.

The postmaster was a gardener by avocation. The night before, he had cut carnations, roses, and leaves. Now he made garlands for each stamp counter and one big wreath for the post-office door. While he was so occupied, seventy-four miles from Tel Aviv, in the Plain of Esdraelon, the Haganah's Gideon Battalion was engaged in trying to take an Arab strong-point, Beisan, which was dominated by a fortified police station. The Jewish commander blocked all the approaches to Beisan and sent a message to its Arab defenders: "You are completely surrounded. If you do not surrender, we will use artillery." His artillery consisted of two three-inch mortars and eight shells, and he knew that an Arab relief force was on its way. On a sudden inspiration, he ordered irrigation pipes placed in "firing positions" and the real mortars to fire a round. His phone rang at once; the Arabs offered to surrender at noon. That would be too late, replied the commander. By 10 A.M., Beisan had surrendered.

At Etzion, however, the entire Jewish garrison, on orders from Tel Aviv, had capitulated to the Transjordanian Arab Legion and was waiting to go into captivity. The Haganah commander had come to Etzion with the last convoy, only to watch its defenses crumble under fire. Had there been no women in Etzion, the men might have risked a break through the hills, still dotted with the cyclamens and poppies of Palestine's brief, brilliant spring. As they waited, the Arabs approached through the hills with shouts of victory. Meanwhile, the Red Cross evacuated the wounded along the road to Jerusalem.

The news of the capture of Beisan reached Tel Aviv at 10 A.M., the last sad message from Etzion at ten past eleven. At headquarters, an order was drafted for the requisitioning of all civilian buses for troop transport. Someone suddenly realized that the old red house on the seashore which had been turned into Haganah headquarters was itself quite unprotected. By this time there were twenty-one old anti-aircraft guns in the whole of Jewish Palestine, and four of these were now trundled into position around the building.

The "Committee of the Situation" was still busy with the proclamation. A secretary ran to the central branch of Tel Aviv's largest bank and started turning out copies on its duplicating machine. Another girl sprinted to a stationery store to buy the pen with which it would be signed. She asked for a gold pen, but had to make do with a gold-plated one.

In the museum, paintings by Jewish artists on Jewish themes had been discreetly substituted for Impressionist nudes, and a portrait of Herzl had been hung. As for parchment for the proclamation, the young graphic artist finally located some synthetic material that seemed suitable. After taking it home and testing it by fire and water in his kitchen sink, he concluded that it would survive for years. There was no time to have it illuminated; it would be signed first, and the agreed text filled in later. A man from the Jewish Agency also suggested that a bank be asked to keep its vault open until after the ceremony.

About twenty minutes to four, two of the Haganah's nine licensed pilots were in the control tower of a small airfield near headquarters in Tel Aviv making bets as to when the Arab invasion would actually start. They were joined by the officer in charge of the airfield, a twenty-three-year-old South African who had come as a volunteer from abroad. He had just returned from a flight over Etzion and had seen the Arab Legion trucks carrying the prisoners to Hebron. He decided to take his Bonanza up again later for a reconnaissance flight from border to border. Meanwhile, he would nap.

In the police station on the border between Arab Jaffa and Jewish Tel Aviv a burly officer read the morning's blotter. No serious crimes—a car stolen, two wrangling women brought in for questioning, a child lost. He glanced at the clock on the wall and turned a page in the blotter. Crossing out the English and Arabic column headings, he wrote in Hebrew: "May 14, 1948. This afternoon we start a new page as members of a Jewish Police Force. All those in station will sign below in honor of this historic date." The eight policemen in the station signed.

At a twenty-one-bed infirmary in Sarona, a nurse rolled bandages, one eye on her watch. A couple of badly wounded Haganah boys had been brought in from near Jerusalem. Facilities at the hospital, whose only doctor came from Tel Aviv several times a day, were primitive. Early that morning she had collected jam jars from her neighbors for the closet-size dispensary. Now it was five minutes to four, and putting aside the bandages, she turned on the radio. So did the people in the Tel Aviv post office, and a Jewish Agency port official awaiting the immigrants who were due to arrive that day from the detention camps on Cyprus.

Outside the museum, crowds had assembled along with representatives of the press, only one of whom was permitted to enter. Inside, the future cabinet members sat at a long table. Facing them were two hundred people—the writers, the artists, the economists, the rabbis, and the Haganah leaders who had played leading roles in the struggle for independence. Ben-Gurion, usually in shirtsleeves and tieless, looked unfamiliar in his dark suit. His voice even, his eyes riveted to the paper he held, he read the proclamation. In 979 Hebrew words, which took less than twenty-two minutes to read, it dealt with the unbroken connection between the Land and the People. It announced that Israel, which was the name chosen for the new state, would be open to all Jews from all the countries of their dispersion. It would uphold freedom of religion, conscience, education, and culture, and would safeguard the holy places. Israel would abide by the UN charter and now called upon the UN for help. Then Ben-Gurion read the final paragraph of the proclamation: "With faith in Almighty God, we set our hands to this Declaration, at this Session of the Provisional State Council, in the City of Tel Aviv, on this Sabbath eve, the fifth day of Iyar, the fourteenth day of May, 1948."

He scheduled the next meeting of the provisional council for Sunday, May 16. "If possible," he added. The traditional Jewish blessing was intoned: "Blessed be Thou, oh Lord our God, King of the Universe, who has kept us alive and made us endure and brought us to this day."

His eyes moist, Ben-Gurion read the first ordinances of the new government. From a gallery upstairs, the Palestine Philharmonic Orchestra played the "Hatikvah." At exactly 4:37½ P.M., he banged a gavel and said, "The State of Israel has arisen. This meeting is ended."

The graphic artist took the signed scroll and raced to the bank, where officials waited to open the vault. The nurse in

Sarona broke a chocolate bar into twenty-one pieces, one for each wounded patient. At a Haganah camp not far from Tel Aviv, a soldier who had spent the day digging trenches on his own, stood at attention while a small plane flew past, dropping copies of the first draft of the proclamation. David Ben-Gurion, alone for a moment, wrote in his diary: "At 4 P.M. the Declaration of Independence. The people are profoundly happy. I am filled with foreboding."

The South African pilot was aloft by 5 P.M. He flew northeast along the Syrian border, down to Jordan and up to Jerusalem, and back to Tel Aviv. What he saw scared him. Hundreds of Arab vehicles moved in convoys along the roads into Israel. These were real armies on the move. In all of the new state, there wasn't a tenth of what he had just seen. Back in Tel Aviv, at 7 P.M., he tore into the operations room at Haganah headquarters. Yadin listened patiently. "We know all this," he said gently.

As the sun set, Tel Aviv was blacked out for the first time since World War II. A tent was set up in the middle of town for sale of the first National Defense Loan. The back page of the evening papers featured the Scripture reading for the day. It was from the prophet Amos: "I will bring back the captives of my people . . . and plant them on their land." All the necessary arrangements had been made, including tea and sandwiches, for the reception of the refugee boat from Cyprus. Most of its passengers were young, and many would go straight into battle. Buses were waiting for them at the port.

In Hebron, at nine o'clock that night, the lights went off in the police station where the Etzion prisoners were lodged. The young Jewish commander settled himself on the tiled floor. An Arab policeman bent down to him, whispering. He was sorry there was nothing to eat, but the prisoners would be taken soon to permanent quarters in Transjordan. Bending lower, he said, "The Jews proclaimed their State this afternoon." The commander closed his eyes and slept.

In Jerusalem, Arieh Ben-Tovim finished his supper of de-
hydrated potatoes and suggested "Etziona" as a name for the
baby about to be born next door. His own children were
asleep in the shelter. Earlier, they had collected bottles from
abandoned houses in a nearby village to be used as Molotov
cocktails when ammunition ran out, as it was bound to soon.
A Haganah message arrived for Arieh. Roadblocks were ur-
gently needed at Meah Shearim, a labyrinth of alleys where
Jerusalem's most pious Jews lived. Arieh mustered forty-eight
bearded, ear-locked men in working squads, giving them in-
structions in Yiddish rather than in Hebrew, the holy tongue
not to be desecrated by common use. They had never worked
on a Sabbath before, but this was a matter of life or death,
and in such cases the Law allowed violation. Gradually, their
work quickened; they began to chant their ancient songs,
and swayed in a semi-dance as they worked.

Martha Black, awakened by the crashing of guns, heard
their singing. God, she confided to her notebook, had told
her that she must stay with the Jews through these terrible
times. Outside her window, she saw the white flowers of an
acacia tree, and a second later, a bullet ricocheted off its
branches. She thanked the Lord for her deliverance, said
her prayers, and went to sleep.

In Haifa, the captain of *H.M.S. Euryalus* checked his
watch; the time was 23:59. In sixty seconds, the cruiser
would start for Britain. Below deck, Sir Alan Cunningham,
too, noted the time. Soon he would leave Palestine, its terrorists and its fanatic population, behind him.

Far south, in the Negev, at a tiny kibbutz called Nirim,
two and a half miles from the Egyptian border, the late night
patrol made its rounds. Barbed wire had been placed all
around the settlement several weeks ago, and it was still
intact. The desert was, as usual at this hour, empty and
black. Two of Nirim's forty-five settlers, out on patrol, looked
at the paling sky and shook hands solemnly. One of them
said, "It's May fifteenth, the first day of the State." They

then went off to check the kibbutz arms store, its four shelters, and the radio transmitter.

The Haganah's main communication center was in a private apartment in Tel Aviv. A half-hour before midnight, a message was picked up from a ham operator in New Jersey. "American Jewry requests Ben-Gurion to broadcast tonight. Awaiting reply." A few hours later, one of the young men who worked the Haganah's clandestine one-kilowatt transmitter rushed to Ben-Gurion's house with a message. "Truman has recognized us!" he yelled. Ben-Gurion, in pajamas, drove to the communications center, where another message was being recorded, confirming the news. He took time to scribble a few words, the connections to the United States were made, and he began to talk.

It was five-twenty in the morning. At five-twenty-five a tremendous noise shook the room. Tel Aviv was being bombed. Ben-Gurion, speaking emphatically, leaned forward: "This noise you hear is the sound of enemy aircraft over our heads." When he finished the broadcast, he was told that the Haganah airfield had been hit. On the way to see what had happened, he met Yigael Yadin and they drove on together.

The South African pilot, in a Tel Aviv hotel for the night, woke up, the drone of Spitfires in his ears. He grabbed a parked jeep and got to the field in three minutes. A bomb had hit the hangar; a hut was burning; the noise was deafening. Ben-Gurion stood in an open car, still in pajamas, watching. The plane came back again, this time hitting part of an adjacent power station. The South African saw the enemy plane circle, lose height, and fly away, a plume of white smoke trailing after it. Jumping into his Bonanza, he took off after it, and within a few minutes caught up with it. The plane had been brought down by anti-aircraft fire near the power station. On a nearby beach he found the Egyptian pilot, lightly wounded. The enemy pilot was taken to headquarters for interrogation, and then driven to the little hospital in Sarona for treatment. He was Israel's first prisoner of war.

By seven o'clock on the first morning of the State of Israel's existence, while the bombardment of Tel Aviv was still going on, the refugees from Cyprus arrived, dressed in their best clothes. Stepping ashore, they saw a banner reading: "Welcome Home!" It had been lettered that night by the young graphic artist when he came back from the museum. An old man waved a slip of paper. "Look!" he said. It read: "The right to settle in the Land of Israel is hereby given." It was signed by "The Immigration Department, Israel." Samuel Brand, aged eighty, held the infant state's first immigration visa.

At 7:30 A.M., David Ben-Gurion, from the window of headquarters, watched the refugee ship come in. He stood, weary, looking out to sea. Yadin walked up to him. His face was grave and so was the news he brought. The full-scale invasion had begun.

The Arabs had attacked Nirim with three hundred men, six-pound guns, and armored cars. At dawn, the country had been penetrated at various points by the armies of Egypt, Lebanon, Syria, Transjordan, and Iraq. Everywhere, the Jews were resisting. Ben-Gurion looked out to sea again. Only twenty-four hours had passed since the High Commissioner had left Government House in Jerusalem. Everything had gone according to schedule so far—the British withdrawal, the establishment of the state, and the war. Whatever happened next, he thought, in those hours just past, the third Jewish commonwealth had become a fact.

The question was: Could it survive its birth?

CHAPTER TEN

THE WAR OF INDEPENDENCE

IsRAEL's War of Independence was fought in fits and starts, in a series of desperate defensive movements alternating with quick, strong attacks on the enemy. It began formally in May, 1948, and ended in June, 1949. But in actual fact it had started months earlier, in November of 1947, with the UN resolution to partition Palestine.

Israel's first line of defense was the green ring of collective settlements and small cooperative villages which dotted all of Palestine's border areas, and which from the beginning of the Return had been planned as outposts. For years, the farmers of the Jewish colonies had struggled against the harsh climate, against the desert, against aridity and erosion. Now the ultimate responsibility for the state's survival rested on them. If they abandoned their farms and fled to the more secure areas of Jewish Palestine, or crumbled before the invading armies which threatened them, the newborn state would surely be lost.

No one knew this better than the farmers of Negba, a small, typically weather-beaten desert settlement with 145 members in all, counting the children. Negba had been founded at the start of the fight against the White Paper and its land restrictions, in the uneasy days of 1939. Its name means "Negevwards," and from its inception it was an oasis in Palestine's parched south, and proof positive that determination and hard work could accomplish the seemingly impossible. Filled with a sense of mission and of adventure, Negba's young pioneers had managed, by 1948, to produce some sixty acres of well-cultivated land. From the cracked, dry soil, they had wrested flourishing orchards and vineyards, and had even launched a tiny factory to turn out the kind of sturdy furniture that other Negev kibbutzim could use.

In the months that preceded the Proclamation of Independence, the people of Negba began to make ready for the war that seemed inevitable. They dug trenches, prepared shelters, and set up a network of primitive first-aid stations and emergency kitchens. They also prepared their children to face weeks, perhaps even months, of siege, for Negba occupied a peculiarly strategic position. In 1948, it lay precisely in what was then the dead center of the Negev—a minute civilian fortress blocking the way to any Egyptian attack on Tel Aviv. If Negba fell to the invading army, all of Israel's south would fall with it.

There was, therefore, no question that Negba must be held, regardless of the cost. In the last days before the Egyptian invasion, the settlers debated a number of vital issues. One was what should be done about the children. It was all very well to hold drills and teach them special games to play in the shelters and explain to the older ones what war was about, in general, and what *this* was was about in particular; but was it fair to the children themselves? The kibbutz took a vote and made a heartbreaking decision— whatever happened to the kibbutz the children would stay on with their parents. No one would leave. But the Haganah High Command decided otherwise, and one night a convoy of darkened buses and armored cars descended on Negba to take all the youngsters away to safety until the war was over.

The pace of work slowed down. The fields were still irrigated, the poultry fed, meals served in the communal dining room, but the normal hustle and bustle of a busy community was silenced. The children were gone. Any day now, the blow would fall; no one knew if the settlement would survive, or which of its members would die before the month of May ended. Negba held its breath, and waited.

At last, on the twenty-third of May, the Egyptians attacked. They hit Negba with everything they had. They attacked with planes, with tanks, with hundreds of infantrymen. The first bomb dropped on the kibbutz put Negba's two machine guns out of commission and killed five of the settlers. The village divided up into a number of small sections, each with its own "commander," its own emergency rations of water and food, its own meager supply of rifles and ammunition. By noon of that day, Negba had become a bloody battlefield and its death toll rose hourly. There seemed to be no chance at all that it could survive. But the kibbutz, or what was left of it, dug in. In the noise and pain and terror of the attack, no one thought dramatic thoughts or composed lofty last-minute statements about courage or resistance, but everyone knew that far more than the fate of one village depended on what would happen before the week was out.

During that week and the ten dreadful weeks that followed the people of Negba showed their mettle. They hurled hand grenades and Molotov cocktails at Egyptian tanks; with a few three-inch mortars, and the help of a handful of Haganah reinforcements sent in before the siege began, they brought down an Egyptian plane and two armoured vehicles. They took long turns defending the village, and in between, cheerfully put out a stenciled bulletin, *The Voice of Negba*, which was sent by carrier pigeon from one outlying trench to another. They conducted elaborate chess tournaments by field telephone, and the women served at least one hot meal every day from the subterranean kitchen.

In the middle of the war, the UN ordered a cease-fire. It had named a Swedish diplomat, Count Folke Bernadotte, as mediator, and it was largely through his efforts that two truces were arranged. Bernadotte, however, was assassinated, probably by Jewish terrorists, who were never identified, and his successor carried on with the arduous job of trying to end the hostilities. The first cease-fire went into effect in June, 1948.

In Negba, some two hundred people came up for air and looked around. The kibbutz was smouldering; not a single house was intact, not a single tractor could ever be used again, and the little cemetery in the back of the village was full. But Negba had survived—and so had Tel Aviv. When the next attack started, Negba went underground again. The Egyptians sent in wave after wave of armored vehicles, artillery, aircraft, and infantry. Negba, wincing, still held fast. At last, arms, ammunition, and the first Israeli planes reached the Negev, and the Egyptians dispersed and withdrew.

It took a year to rebuild Negba, to put up a new water tower, a new barn, and new houses. But Negba's children came home a few days after the offensive had been repelled and the kibbutz went back to battling its real enemy, the desert. That was the way the War of Independence went in most places, but not everywhere. Along with its 6,000 dead, Israel sustained several losses of territory, and one of them was the Old City of Jerusalem.

Jerusalem—capital of David's kingdom, the city in which Jesus had been crucified and from which, according to ancient legend, Mohammed had risen on his black steed to Heaven—had a total Jewish population of 90,000 in 1948, almost all of it located in the New City. But within the walls of the Old City, now held by the Arabs, there still lived 1,500 residents of the Jewish Quarter. Most of them were Orthodox Jews, whose attachment to the Old City stemmed from the very antiquity and sacredness of its cobbled lanes and high ramparts. For them, the New City was largely an intrusive presence, a secular reminder that the Jews of Israel were not motivated primarily by a simple religious faith like theirs. The Holy Land was where they awaited the coming of the

Messiah, and in that Land there was no holier place than Jerusalem, and the core and heart of Jerusalem was the Old City.

All of Jerusalem, both Old and New, had been cut off for weeks by the Arab siege. Then suddenly, accidentally, a way had been found to reach the coastal plain—a dusty bypass, winding over the mountains—and again Jerusalem was linked with Tel Aviv. Hundreds of people, most of them men too old to fight, volunteered to form a human chain; nightly, making their way in single file through the hills, they hauled sixty-pound loads of cement and light arms on their backs. Combat engineers and other volunteers roughed out the path and widened it, moving rocks and stones, until, bit by bit the historic route became a rocky road. It was formally named the Road of Valour, but dubbed the Burma Road, after the World War II route along which goods were transported to China. Many of the workers were new immigrants, fresh from the detention camps at Cyprus; stumbling, night after night, across the little "Burma Road," they broke the siege of Jerusalem.

But in a small part of the Old City, hundreds of Jews still huddled, terrified, in tiny groups, the target of incessant Arab Legion shelling, watching the Jewish Quarter go up in flames, and facing the possibility of capture. Elsewhere in Israel, it was win or perish. In the Old City, however, where the Arab Legion and Iraqi soldiers commanded the very walls and held the city's seven ancient gates, there seemed to be no alternative to surrender. The price for the defense of the Jewish Quarter would have been hundreds of young Israeli lives and the destruction of the cupolas, minarets, and shrines of the Holy Places which had stood for so many years and had witnessed so much of human history.

Was it worth it? Was even the Wailing Wall worth the stupendous human cost? In Tel Aviv, the Haganah High Command finally took an anguished stand. Let the Jewish Quarter fall! And fall it did, to Jordan's Arab Legion. The old people and the children were evacuated and allowed to cross into the New City, but the survivors of the bitter hand-to-hand fighting that had raged in the Jewish Quarter for more than two weeks were taken, dazed and unbelieving, into captivity. The Jewish Quarter, ruined, was blown up by the Legion, and the battle for Jerusalem ended. Those who had lived through the surrender swore that one day they would return to the Old City, and many of them would do so in 1967, nineteen years in the future.

By the autumn of 1949, Israel's War of Independence was over. More than a thousand square miles had been added to the territory of the Jewish state. The Arabs no longer threatened Tel Aviv, Haifa, and the coastal plain. The road to Jerusalem had been widened and secured, and the New City was declared the capital of Israel. The main Arab bases in the Galilee had been wiped out, and the Israelis, moving swiftly southwards, backed by their small air force and a few tanks, had smashed their way deep into the Negev, linking it with the rest of the state. Israel Army units raised Israel's flag over Eilat, on the southernmost tip of the Gulf of Aqaba, which once had served as harbor for Solomon's merchant fleet, and which now gave Israel an outlet to Africa and the Orient. Her borders were still not easy to defend, but even a precarious peace was better than none at all, and would permit the state to grow and develop. At least Ben-Gurion's question had been answered. The infant state had lived through the violent night of its birth.

The Arabs and the Jews signed armistice agreements. The Arab states had done badly in the war. Only Jordan managed to wrench land away from the Israelis, adding some 2,000 square miles of Palestine to its kingdom. No one talked of the stillborn Arab state, planned by the UN, which might have come into being. The Egyptians, the Syrians, the Iraqis, and the Lebanese began talking about a second round. But what really mattered was that the war was finished, and that Israel, very much an established fact, could at last turn her attention to the complicated problems of statehood.

The provisional government which had directed the war, levied the first taxes, and set up the first administrative agencies now became a permanent government. National elections were held in January, 1949, and a constituent assembly—the Knesset—met in solemn conclave a month later to install a president and honor its first prime minister, David Ben-Gurion, who had led the nation to victory.

The choice of Israel's first president was not difficult. Aging and half blind, Dr. Chaim Weizmann had nonetheless played an active role in the international negotiations which preceded the establishment of the state. If anyone could be called Israel's Grand Old Man, it was without doubt this frail, distinguished scientist-turned-statesman. During most of the war, Dr. Weizmann had been busy abroad. Now Israel's fledgling Air Transport Command was officially requested to fly the President-designate from Geneva to Lydda. It was its first formal civilian mission, and it was decided that the "airline" must be given a name. It was called *El Al* ("To the Skies"), and a flying camel was chosen as its emblem. On the tail fin of the Presidential aircraft, official-looking but absolutely meaningless letters were painted so that it would look more impressive; no one ever knew exactly why "4X-ACA" had been chosen. In the same spirit of keeping up appearances, a team of brand-new customs inspectors and passport control officers were stationed at Lydda airport, although the customs had not yet been organized in Israel. A crew and a stewardess, their uniforms hastily designed and sewn in Tel Aviv, were assigned to the DC-4. At Lydda, an armed guard greeted the President-designate and his wife. Then, the amenities disposed of, the DC-4 was stripped of its finery and returned that same day to serve in the Air Transport Command.

In May, 1949, Israel was accepted as a member of the United Nations. That summer, the first ambassadors arrived, those of the United States and of the U.S.S.R. Because the

UN had refused to accept Jerusalem as the capital of the new state and still demanded its internationalization according to the original plan, the two ambassadors were stationed in Tel Aviv. The war was still on and no residences were ready for them. They stayed in a small Tel Aviv hotel, in rooms that lacked telephones, and all their confidential official business was conducted in their respective bathrooms, which could be securely locked.

One center of attraction for all of the foreign diplomats and for most Israelis that year was Parliament itself. A Tel Aviv movie house had been quickly refurbished and air-conditioned, and in it the 120 members of the Knesset passed the state's first laws. The most dramatic of these ordinances, and one of the first to be enacted, was the Law of Return, which stipulated that the gates of Israel were open to any Jew from anywhere, regardless of his financial, social, educational, or physical condition, and conferred Israeli nationality on every Jew desiring to enter Israel as an immigrant. The Proclamation of Independence had already declared that "the State of Israel will be open to Jewish immigration and the ingathering of the exiles," and now this became the law of the land.

In the first eighteen months of the state's existence, 341,000 Jews arrived in Israel. Some came at the very height of the war and those who were healthy enough went from ship to shore and right into army units. They came from all over the world, from every country which had a Jewish population of any size at all. Some were the remnants of European Jewry. Some came from as far as China. Still others came from Libya, from Bulgaria, from Morocco. They came in torrents, in the hundreds and thousands, by ship and by plane, and by the end of 1951, the Jewish population of Israel had doubled.

One of the largest single groups from any one country were the Jews of Iraq, many of them undoubtedly direct descendants of those Jews who had gone into exile in Babylon two thousand years earlier. They arrived in a series of giant airlifts, called "Operation Ali Baba," 124,225 of them, almost 93 per cent of the total Jewish population of Iraq. The most touching and most spectacular of the mass immigrations was that of the Jews of Yemen. They had lived in a backward Moslem monarchy on the southwest coast of Arabia, probably since the days of King Solomon. In the very beginning of the Zionist settlement of Palestine some Yemenite Jews, hearing of the return to the Holy Land, had walked across the deserts until they reached Palestine, but they were few in number.

Over the centuries, the Yemenite Jews had been treated as second-class citizens, but they had never lost faith in their eventual redemption. In 1948, receiving word of the establishment of Israel, they started to leave Yemen. Miraculously, they endured the long trek south across the deserts and through the high dangerous mountain passes of Arabia, to say nothing of the raids of robber bands and the depredations of the various small sultanates that lay on the land route to Aden. In Aden, then a British protectorate, the Yemenites waited placidly for the Lord to bring them to Zion on the wings of eagles, as it is written in the Bible.

Soon news reached Israel of the amazing exodus, and a massive airlift was organized. The Israelis named it "Operation Magic Carpet," but the Yemenite Jews looked up at the planes that had come to take them home and believed that truly these were eagles' wings. The converted World War II transport planes flew 45,000 Yemenite Jews to Lydda, and so small and emaciated were the passengers that as many as 130 of them were carried in a single plane. Each family had paid a head tax to the Imam of Yemen for permission to leave; each family had brought its most treasured possession, the Bible scrolls, and had strange tales to tell of the journey on foot to Aden.

In Yemen, these Jews had maintained their own culture. They spoke Arabic, but all the boys were taught Hebrew.

Because the Hebrew school was too poor to have more than one copy of the Bible, they learned to read from all angles, upside down and sideways, and all of them knew the Old Testament by heart. The Yemenite Jews were craftsmen, excelling as silversmiths and goldsmiths, but they were ready to do anything and learned rapidly. They rejoiced in their Israeli identity cards and in the knowledge that they were now first-class citizens, and nothing was too hard for them in their new home. They gave to Israel their gentle, centuries-old traditions, their ability to work diligently and without complaint, and their quick, bright intelligence.

Somehow, all the thousands of immigrants had to be fed and housed; somehow they had to be integrated into the economy of a new country which was still at war. The Jewish Agency, aided by world Jewry, faced up to the stupendous job. Tent cities sprang up all over Israel, gradually to be replaced by ugly, but temporary, shanty towns made up of dozens of small, crowded, tin huts. They were not pretty, but they gave shelter to the immigrants, and each family was provided with the bare essentials, with food, furniture, and clothing.

The melting pot simmered. Thrown higgledy-piggledy together, Jews from Bucharest and Constantinople, from Shanghai and Georgia, from the wild Atlas Mountains and the ghettos of Tunisia worked and lived, often in unbearably close proximity. Many of the immigrants were not well enough to hold down jobs or help support their families, and special hospitals were set up to provide for the hundreds who were chronically sick and disabled.

There was also the problem of language. Jews from seventy-four countries had streamed into Israel. They spoke Arabic, Yiddish, French, Russian, Polish, and a score of other tongues, but they lacked a common language. If the revival of Biblical Hebrew ever needed justification, it was magnificently justified now. Hebrew became the most important single factor uniting the Jews of Israel. Hundreds of *ulpanim*, special schools equipped to teach the language rapidly, opened all over the country. The radio and the daily press ran special features for Hebrew beginners. The school system was expanded to make room for thousands of children who had to start from scratch. Even the Israel Defense Forces laid stress on the teaching of Hebrew, and to some extent, in those first stormy years, the army also became a school in which thousands of young immigrants learned to master their new language.

The army had emerged from the underground into broad daylight. It was one thing to be a dedicated soldier in a partisan force in which military discipline, though tight enough, had few external expressions, and something else to be part of a regular army, with organized ranks, uniforms, and definite periods of service. In most armies, military codes develop through the generations; in the army of Israel, however, they had to be created almost at once. The army turned for its doctrines and concepts to its own past, to the code of the Haganah. It would remain a skilled, well-trained, and highly mobile force, able, whenever necessary, to pack a considerable punch. It did away with many of the traditions which existed in older armies. There was a minimum of saluting, and virtually no difference either in pay or the standard of living for officers and enlisted men. Most important, it determined to remain basically a civilian army. The small regular army consisted primarily of officers and noncommissioned officers. The other soldiers, men and women alike, were in the reserves from the time they were twenty until they were forty-five, serving at least one month a year. As someone put it, they were soldiers on an eleven-month annual leave each year. Also, all eighteen-year-olds were obliged to do two to three years of military service, and then they, too, became part of the reserves.

From the beginning, from 1949, there was no difference between the soldier on active service and the soldier in the reserves, always prepared for an emergency call-up. Everyone got the same intense, tough training. But the army found time to help with the mass immigration as well, aided greatly in the setting-up of the *ma'abarot*, or transient immigrant camps, and did what it could to make the conditions easier for the new immigrants, including teaching thousands to read and write.

Life was not easy for anyone in Israel from 1948 to 1952. To begin with, thrown back wholly on its own resources and suffering the economic results of a world-wide Arab blockade, Israel suddenly had to fend for itself on a number of fronts. Food was scarce; so was money. As the immigrants poured in, the little which the original community of 600,000 had possessed by way of income or property now had to be sliced into a great many more pieces. It was a time of austerity (*tsena* in Hebrew), and Israelis learned to make do with very little. But making do was not enough; jobs had to be found for the newcomers and food had to be grown.

Israel wearily flexed its muscles and got down to work. Scaffolding went up everywhere, and the country hummed with construction projects. New settlements—some two hundred in the course of the state's first eighteen months—were established. Thousands of acres of newly irrigated land gradually helped fill the national breadbasket, and industry kept pace. Scores of factories were set up, and Israel began to manufacture her own heavy machinery for agricultural use. In Tel Aviv and Jerusalem, governmental planners looked for every possible way of lessening the country's dependence on the world outside. One of the more complicated projects was to search out, classify, and exploit whatever natural resources Israel could claim. Guided partly by the Bible, teams of surveyors, geochemists, and archaeologists combed the state, in particular the Negev, for minerals, and came up with a fairly impressive list. Copper, iron ore, and manganese were located, as were phosphorus and even a little oil.

Whole networks of roads and highways were constructed.

Some were for defense purposes; other facilitated the delivery of the country's products to the harbors, which were themselves improved and developed. Israelis tightened their belts, queued up for meager weekly rations of food, and grumbled loudly about inadequate housing. But no one had promised that independence would be easy, or that it would be simple to keep Israel from collapsing under the triple burden of battle, boycott, and almost a million new citizens. Only time would tell whether the burden was indeed too great.

CHAPTER ELEVEN

Israel's First Decade

In 1958, Israel celebrated her tenth birthday. The holiday was celebrated throughout the nation with deeply felt emotion; everywhere there were gala parades and parties. Between the festivities, the people took time out to look back and assess their accomplishments, and the most important single fact to emerge was that Israel had survived her first decade, a strenuous decade of hardship and war.

Those ten years had changed the face of the country. Tel Aviv, Haifa, Jerusalem had all become large cities, by any standard, and a crop of smaller towns had sprouted everywhere, mostly in the south. Some of them, like Dimona and Mitzpeh Ramon, were brand-new; others, like Beersheba and Eilat, were rooted in antiquity but had come to life again. The new development towns were all very much alike —dry, dusty, bursting at the seams with energy. They had made the transition from drawing-board to reality with a breathtaking speed which left no time for preening or primping, and in the main, like most frontier towns, they were not very attractive.

The new immigrants now went straight from the quay to permanent housing. The rate of Israel's growth had not slowed down much since 1948, and by 1958 the population had almost trebled. But the process of integration had speeded up a great deal. It was becoming harder and harder to tell the difference between children whose parents had come to Israel from Yemen or India or Bulgaria and the "sabra," or native-born Israeli. Home life was usually still very much colored by the children's respective backgrounds. Mothers from Yugoslavia, the United States, and France served different food, sang different songs, and told different stories. Family celebrations varied. The customs of Moroccan Jews, for example, in no way resembled those of Australian Jews, and weddings, birthdays, funerals, and religious holidays all had their own slightly different flavor. But outside the home, the gaps were beginning to close. Israeli children all had the same kind of names; almost all of them derived from the Bible, as did most of the place names of Israel's towns and villages. The average school roll call sounded as though it were made up of Old Testament figures—Avital, Yoram, Naomi, Judith, and David.

The Bible, in fact, served as a very sturdy link between all the cultures which had come together in the new state. Although there were two kinds of schools in Israel, one of which placed greater emphasis on religion and the traditions of Judaism, all school children learned the Bible thoroughly. It served them not only as a source book for the language they spoke, but also as a text for geography, history, botany, and literature. Elementary school was, of course, compulsory. Children from five to fourteen were educated at the state's expense. In the early years, Israel lacked sufficient schoolrooms, teachers, and equipment for the hundreds of new pupils, and in many of the immigrant reception camps children learned arithmetic and English in tents, writing on planks propped up by stones.

After school, Israel's children did very much what children all over the world do in their leisure time; they read, went to movies, listened to the radio, and played football. One rather special feature was the youth movements, which were affiliated with political parties and combined scout training and plain fun with lectures on current events and Israel's social and economic problems. Another distinction between the activities of Israel's youngsters and their counterparts abroad was that all children in high school received some brief basic military training. It was usually only for an hour or so a week, but since they would go into the army as soon as they graduated, this early toughening-up process was considered essential. A third, though more trivial, difference was Israel's six-day week. The country was poor as well as small, and Saturday, the Sabbath, was the only day of rest. The school week was, therefore, a long one.

Some of the changes that had taken place in Israel since the War of Independence were crucial. In 1948 some 900,000 Arabs had lived in Palestine, and even before the War of Independence broke out officially, the propagandists of the Arab national movement began a full-scale radio campaign to convince the Palestinian Arabs that they should leave their homes. Day after day, the Arabs were told by their leaders to retreat until the war against the Jews ended; day after day they were assured, in vivid phrases and with considerable dramatic flair, that the Jews would be driven into the sea and that then all Palestine would belong to them. Jewish homes and Jewish farms would be theirs for the taking; all the abundance of the Jewish National Home would pass into the hands of the country's rightful owners.

The Arab leaders also announced that those who disobeyed their orders and remained in Palestine would be regarded as traitors. The credulous Arabs, bewildered and frightened, began to flee to adjoining Arab territory. Whether they were victims of mass hysteria, herd psychology, or simple fear, the fact is that by the time the War of Independence was over, about 570,000 Arabs had abandoned their villages and run away. The Arab states denied them even a minimum of consideration, refusing to give them either citizenship or work permits. The refugees were forced to live under miserable conditions in special camps set up along Israel's borders. The UN fed the refugees, educated their children, and saw to it that some standard of public health was maintained in the crowded camps.

As it turned out, the Arab states themselves found the refugee camps very useful. First of all, they were a constant reproach to the world in general and to the Jews in particular; secondly, they were a potential fifth column which seethed with hatred for Israel and was responsive to agitation and incitement. Every now and then, terrorist groups, made up of these Palestinian Arabs, were formed and trained to attack Israel. In the course of time, their effectiveness grew, and the early 1950's began to resemble the 1930's in Israel, in terms of sabotage, violence, and murder. The Arab states denied any connection with the guerilla warfare and said that they were doing their best to discourage it, but the terrorist bands were still being equipped with arms and taught to infiltrate Israel's frontiers.

Not all the Arabs became refugees; 230,000 stayed in Israel. In some respects, they had a difficult time. The Israeli drive toward progress and Westernization, which quickened the tempo of life, placed great pressure on the Arabs who felt themselves aliens in a familiar land. The Government of Israel, recognizing this, decided from the outset not to disturb the traditional Arab way of life more than necessary. Arab children continued to attend Arab schools, often knew no Hebrew at all, and, except in the few towns which had mixed populations, kept very much to themselves. Arabic, however, was one of Israel's two official languages. The Arabs ran their own religious courts, had full political equality, and formed their own political parties. They were elected to the Knesset and could become members of the General Federation of Labor.

The economic situation of the Israeli Arabs was better than that of most Arabs elsewhere, and they learned to take full advantage of modern methods of agriculture and irrigation. Their villages prospered through the years and their health improved beyond recognition. Israel boasted of one doctor for every two hundred inhabitants—the highest ratio of any country—and Arab infant mortality in Israel became the lowest in the Arab world. Still, the Arabs were now a minority—a large one, it is true, but a minority nonetheless, and because the security situation remained tense, with the Arab states stubbornly rejecting any suggestion of signing peace treaties with Israel, the government kept a cautious eye on the Arab population.

Besides the Arabs (most of whom were Moslems, though there were some 52,000 Christian Arabs as well), Israel found herself responsible for a variety of other minorities, some of them very small and exotic. There were, for example, some 2,000 Circassians, whose Russian ancestors had converted from Christianity to Islam in the seventeenth century. Another group was the Druses, who lived in about twenty villages, mainly in the north, and who, though they spoke Arabic, were not Moslems. Their religion is a secret one, and its tenets are never revealed to outsiders, but the Druses had suffered for years under Moslem persecution and were greatly relieved to become part of a Jewish state. They became the first minority group to ask that its young men be drafted into the Israel Defense Forces, where they served with valor.

The smallest of all the minority groups was perhaps the best known—the few hundred remaining Samaritans, direct descendants of settlers sent to the Holy Land by the King of Assyria in 722 B.C., when Assyria occupied ancient Israel. The Samaritans have remained apart from both the Jews and the Moslems. Some of their religious practices are Jewish in origin, but they have their own High Priest and worship in their own way.

Less exotic were the country's Christians, of whom there were about 53,000, including representatives of various religious communities and monastic orders. Nuns and monks from every known Christian sect and from all over the world were part of the Israeli scene, especially in Jerusalem; and Christians continued to be the custodians of their own Holy Places throughout Israel.

By the 1950's, there could be no doubt that the complicated social experiment was working. Now and then, the lid flew off the pressure cooker—the Arabs complained that they were being discriminated against, the Orthodox Jews protested everyone else's lack of piety, the Jews from the Arab countries felt that they were not being given an equal chance for advancement with Jews who had immigrated from more advanced lands. But the periodic rumblings always faded away, and bit by bit the Israeli nation, formed by the ingathering of exiles, came into being. The true strength of the new nation was tested when a second war was forced on Israel even before she celebrated her tenth birthday. That war was the Sinai Campaign, and the story behind it began long before the formal starting date of October 29, 1956.

Early in 1955, the terrorist bands plaguing Israel began to step up their operations. The Egyptian government openly sponsored the terrorists and helped organize them in a new "army" whose soldiers were known as the *Fedayeen*. The Fedayeen operated from the so-called Gaza Strip, the territory between Egypt and Israel which, according to the 1949 armistice agreements, was supposed to be a demilitarized zone. But it was there that the Fedayeen headquarters were set up, while smaller bases were established in the other Arab states which bordered Israel.

Now that they had some real support, the infiltrators became more daring. They penetrated deep into Israel, mined roads and vehicles, blew up homes, and killed over 400 Israelis. Occasionally, the Israeli Defense Forces staged retaliatory and warning raids but these, though temporarily effective, failed to stop the undeclared war. Life in Israel became increasingly dangerous.

In the kibbutzim of the Negev, settlers returned unhappily to familiar routines. Lawns were again torn up for trenches, shelters were set up, underground aid posts and bunkers were in almost daily use. Nothing was safe—not people, nor cattle, nor cowsheds. Plowing often had to be done at night and the farmers took turns standing intensified guard duty against the infiltrators. Arms and planes, mostly from the Soviet Union, poured into the Arab states all through 1955, and although some of these weapons were obviously transferred to the Fedayeen, most of them were not. The question was: Against whom were the Arab states arming in such deadly earnest?

In the beginning of 1956, the president of Egypt, Gamal Abdel Nasser, partly answered the question. Speaking in public, he promised the Egyptians that "Palestine" would soon be conquered. By the spring, there were clear indications that Egypt was readying itself for the promised second round. One other significant event took place in the summer. President Nasser, in the face of world opinion and in defiance of international law, seized and nationalized the Suez Canal. Israeli shipping had always been barred from the Canal, although the ban was illegal. The new move made clear that Nasser was really on the warpath, not only against Israel, but also against France and England, both of whom had major interests in the Middle East and particularly in the Suez Canal upon which, to some measure, their economic lives then depended. At the same time, Nasser intensified his blockade of the Gulf of Aqaba, thus critically threatening the security of Israel's southern port, Eilat.

Israelis tried to dismiss the war clouds as a passing phenomenon; it seemed impossible that the state, all of eight years old, would have to fight for its life again. Everyone was tired; everyone hoped against hope that peace, lasting and firm, was around the corner. The immigrants from Cochin China, from Syria, from Poland wanted to relax; they needed to forget the past, attend to the present, and plan the future.

They wanted telephones, cars, milking machines, and combines—the things that were still scarce in Israel and which would make their lives easier and their work more productive. They wanted, in short, to be left alone to work, and the idea of another war was anathema.

Nevertheless, in October the political barometer dropped ominously. Egypt, Jordan, Syria, and Saudi Arabia united in a joint defense pact, placing their armies under President Nasser's command. Large concentrations of Egyptian troops, armor, and artillery began to assemble in the Sinai Peninsula. The signs of war were unmistakable.

The Israelis realized that the next move was up to them. Prime Minister Ben-Gurion, who was also Israel's Minister of Defense, and his Chief of Staff, Moshe Dayan, decided to deny Nasser the luxury of choosing the time and place of his attack. Israel had three primary aims—to deliver a mortal blow to Egypt's strength and to her prestige in the Arab world as a major military power; to wipe out the Fedayeen nests; and to open the Suez Canal and the Gulf of Aqaba to Israeli shipping. Only a surprise assault could accomplish these aims; the Egyptian army's superiority in arms, equipment, and men was enormous. But David had prevailed against Goliath before, and now he would attempt it again.

The prime requisite for surprise is, of course, secrecy. On October 25, 1956, the call-up of the Israel Army reserves began. It went on for four days and nights, silently, almost imperceptibly. The system was simple and effective. A knock at the door, a ring on the phone, a message left with neighbors, a telegram delivered; that was all it took for much of the country's male population to turn into the battalions of well-trained, disciplined soldiers who were to win so brilliant a victory over the Egyptians within a few days. With no explanation to anyone, with just a shrug and a hasty search for the uniform which had been packed away, husbands, sons, and fathers went off to join their units. In four days and nights, barbers, chefs, office clerks, and teachers disappeared from their homes and jobs, and the towns and cities of Israel were emptied of their men. But more than soldiers are needed for war. Buses began to be in short supply, cars and trucks vanished from the streets. Nobody asked questions, but everyone understood. This was it, once again.

The Sinai Campaign began right in the heart of the Sinai Peninsula, less than forty miles from the Suez Canal and the vast Suez bases of the Egyptian army, at a break in the mountains called the Mitla Pass. Here, parachutists were dropped to join up with the infantry brigades. The linking up of the two forces gave Israel its second initial advantage. The first was the sheer unexpectedness and bravado of the attack itself. The battle on land became a battle in the air as well. Despite the size of the Egyptian forces, the Israelis hammered forward, pressing on into enemy territory. It looked as though nothing could stop them, although casualties mounted.

By the fourth day of the campaign, they had traveled farther and faster over cruel and unfamiliar desert terrain than any other combat body had ever done. Driven by the certainty that the alternative to victory was liquidation, the Israeli force, taking with it thousands of prisoners and massive booty, swept through the whole peninsula, while the Egyptians broke ranks, turned tail, and fled. One part of the Israeli army raced on towards the Suez Canal itself, another headed towards the Gaza Strip. A third part pushed on, across deep sand and terrifyingly steep cliffs, to Sharm el Sheikh, on the southernmost tip of the Sinai Peninsula, the Egyptian stronghold from which the blockade of the Gulf of Aqaba had been maintained.

The Israelis reached Sharm el Sheikh on the fifth of November, and took it. They had covered 700 miles and done away with the last of the Egyptian defenses. The whole of the Sinai Peninsula was now in their hands. The war had lasted seven days, and it had resulted in the total defeat of Nasser's army, and in the conquest of an area almost three times the size of Israel itself. Israel's civilian army got ready to put its uniforms away; the mail carrier, the shoemaker, the bank clerk, and the garage mechanic handed back their guns and went home. But there was still a big job to be done. Thousands of Egyptian prisoners had to be returned as soon as possible; immense stores of booty, most of it made in Russia—tanks, trucks, arms, and gigantic quantities of food, clothing, and petrol found in the desert—had to be sorted out; and an occupation force had to be established in the captured territories.

There was one more complication; at the last minute, Israel had acquired allies. On October 30, France and Britain, eager to settle their own scores with Nasser and to get the canal back, decided that the Israel Defense Forces might be very helpful to them in this respect. Their stated pretext for entering the Sinai war was that they would act as referees; they would, they said, separate the combatants and force a cease-fire on everyone. Accordingly, an Anglo-French ultimatum was issued to the Israelis and the Egyptians demanding that both sides vacate the canal area at once. Both sides ignored the ultimatum, and on October 31, the French and British began to bombard Egypt from the air. By the end of that week, they had entered Port Said.

Although the French lent Israel some air cover during the campaign, the intervention was in many ways unfortunate for Israel. It confused the issues and permitted Nasser to raise a hue and cry which was taken up by the rest of the world. He had been unfairly attacked, he claimed, by three aggressor nations, and all three must leave Egyptian territory at once.

In New York, the United Nations convened in an all-night emergency meeting. The British and French conspiracy was loudly condemned, and so was Israel's strike against Nasser. The spokesmen for fifty-seven nations told everyone to clear out of Egypt, and the Israelis were ordered to retreat. The British and French collaboration had actually been both weak and unsuccessful, and the two large powers were somewhat relieved to be extricated from a situation which was not especially to their credit. But the Israelis knew that holding on to the Sinai Peninsula was their only guarantee for future peace, and they tried hard to stay put.

The United Nations, led largely by Russia and the United States, persisted. Pressure and even threats were brought to bear on Israel. Nasser's joy was unconcealed. By its stand, the United Nations turned the Egyptian collapse into a kind of moral victory, and the awkward position of the French and British added to Nasser's glee. The Egyptian people, living under a dictatorship with only state-controlled news available to them, knew nothing of the actual disaster that had befallen them in the desert, nor that their forces had been put to flight. They were to learn the results of the war only much later. Meanwhile, Cairo celebrated the Anglo-French fiasco and waited for the Israelis to pull out.

On the ninth of November, heavy-hearted and apprehensive, the government of Israel finally accepted the United Nations directive and announced that the Israel Army would withdraw as soon as a UN Emergency Force took over to police the Israel-Egyptian frontiers. Once again, there was no alternative. The Israelis moved out of the Sinai Peninsula, out of Sharm el Sheikh, and out of the Gaza Strip.

The war, although it had failed to guarantee a peace, had nonetheless accomplished its main goals. The Fedayeen bases had been destroyed, the Egyptian military machine had been rendered useless, at least for a very long time, and Israel's borders were tranquil again. The blockade of Eilat had been ended. What was more important, the Egyptians had been given notice that Israel was not, and was unlikely to become, a sitting duck, submitting to armed attack.

Israel went back to draining swamps, doing scientific research, baking bread, and conducting archaeological digs—in fact, back to earning a living and to hoping that this might be the last war she would ever have to fight.

CHAPTER TWELVE

Encounters With History

In 1967, when the Six Day War broke out, the State of
Israel faced the most serious threat to its survival. The threat
was overcome mainly because of the will to endure of the
two and a half million Israelis who now made up the nation's population. But the will to live, and to live in freedom,
whatever its price, are not always inherent qualities; especially in so small a country, and in one so recently independent. That Israel did indeed feel itself to be one nation
indivisible, and that it decided to take its destiny into its
own hands and fight for honor and liberty was, in a way, the
result of three major events which had occurred since 1958.
All three of these national experiences nourished and strengthened the sense of Israel's unity; all three, although different,
deepened the awareness of a common past and, even more
significant, of a common future; and all three were part of a
heritage shared alike by the "sabra," born to the land, and
by the immigrant who had made it his.

The first of these lay in the realm of rediscovering the
past—the excavation of Massada. The story of the heroic
defense of Massada was known to every schoolchild in Israel
long before the big dig began. The facts are epic: on a rock
rising nearly 1,500 feet above the Dead Sea, Herod the

Great, about 37 B.C., had built a splendid fortress designed to be used as a luxurious haven in the event of attack. It had pavilions, vast hanging gardens, mosaic floors, and marble baths. To make it impregnable, huge cisterns and massive storerooms were cut into the sheer walls of the cliffs on top of which the strange palace had been erected.

Not many years afterwards, in A.D. 66, massive revolts broke out against the Romans all over Palestine. A group of Jews belonging to the Zealot sect stormed the palace of Massada, wiped out the small Roman garrison stationed there, and took over the mountain fortress. The wars of the Jews against the Romans lasted for four hopeless years, until, in A.D. 70, the Tenth Roman Legion smashed the rebellion and captured Jerusalem. The Temple was razed to the ground, and hundreds of thousands of Jews were sold as slaves and sent into exile. But on the great flat-topped rock of Massada, the Jews made a last symbolic stand; there, 960 men, women, and children defied the might of Rome.

Led by Eleazar Ben Yair, they turned Herod's magnificent mansions into the headquarters of a tiny, besieged community. They stuck it out for three years. Then, in A.D. 73, a large Roman army launched the final assault against the rock; dragging giant catapults and battering rams across the desert, building a siege wall all around Massada so that its defenders could not escape, and erecting a ramp which led to the very top. The Roman general then ordered his troops to attack the fortress with burning brands.

That night, huddled inside the walls, the Zealots made a dramatic decision. They would kill themselves rather than die at Roman hands. They drew lots to determine which men should kill the others so that in the end, when the Romans scaled Massada, battering their way into its halls, they found all but two of the defenders dead, bound in a historic suicide pact.

The excavation of Massada (whose Hebrew name, *Metzuda,* means "stronghold") began in the 1960's. Eventually, almost all of the buildings on the mountain would be cleared, some reconstructed, and a small part of the fortress left intact, exactly as it had been during the revolt of the Jews. Archaeology—the search for the past and for the concrete evidence linking it to the present and to the future—had been a national hobby in Israel for many years, but the saga of Massada stirred the nation's imagination as nothing else had done before.

Month by month, the treasure trove grew, extricated carefully from between the walls and beneath the floors. Bit by bit, the precious details of the defense of Massada were uncovered, mostly by volunteers from Israel and abroad. The finds ranged from cooking pots and coins to priceless Biblical scrolls from a synagogue the Zealots had built on Massada, the only one remaining from Temple times. There were arrows and potsherds, some of them probably used by Ben Yair himself when the fatal lots were drawn, hundreds of parchment fragments, and bones.

The pieces of parchment were perhaps the most significant of all the Massada finds. They included parts of the Book of Genesis, of Deuteronomy, and of the Psalms. Like the famous Dead Sea Scrolls, found years earlier, these fragments were written in exactly the same Hebrew now in use in Israel; one piece of parchment, in fact, was part of a scroll identical with a Dead Sea Scroll. The bronze and silver coins, of which there were hundreds, also dated back to the era of the Jewish insurrection, and many of them were inscribed with the words "For the Freedom of Zion."

Week in, week out, Israelis streamed to Massada. Interest in Massada was inexhaustible. Professor Yigael Yadin, who had once been the Israel Army Chief of Staff and who directed the Massada excavation, was now in constant demand as a lecturer and writer. No matter how hard the day's work, in the evenings people in almost every town and village flocked to hear talks on some new aspect of the Massada story and to stare, never sated, at slides of the prizes found there. In

147

the end, Massada came to be as much a symbol of the present as of the past, and it served as a powerful force uniting the people of so many origins who had come to the Jewish state.

In 1960, the people of Israel became profoundly involved in another, far more tragic and much more recent period of their history. Rising in the Knesset, on a sunny May afternoon, Prime Minister David Ben-Gurion, his face stern, curtly told the nation that Adolph Eichmann, the Nazi, one of the men most directly responsible for carrying out the extermination of six million Jews, had been found, and was already under arrest in Israel. Silently, the Knesset heard Ben-Gurion announce that Eichmann had been positively identified and that he would be charged and put on trial according to the due processes of law.

Behind the Prime Minister's terse statement that afternoon lay a remarkable and still not entirely revealed story of persistence and adventure. In 1945, Ben-Gurion had authorized the Haganah security services to begin a search for some of the more infamous of the many Nazi leaders who had survived the war. The dragnet was cast throughout the world. Wherever notorious S.S. men, involved in the liquidation of Jews, sought refuge, the Haganah, painstakingly picking up clues, following hints and rumors, began to track them down.

Adolph Eichmann, in common with many of his erstwhile colleagues, had gone underground when World War II ended. Patiently, doggedly, the Israeli agents trailed their quarry, first to the continent of South America, and then to Buenos Aires, the capital of Argentina. Eichmann had changed his name and partially altered his appearance. For years he had been living the tranquil life of a typical suburbanite. Now justice closed in on him. Rapidly checking the accumulating evidence, verifying one minute fact after another, the agents of Israel finally tracked him down. Drugged and passive, Adolph Eichmann, who had played a major role in Hitler's terrible "final solution," was put aboard an Israeli aircraft and flown to a secret prison in Israel.

The purposes of the manhunt were complex. To begin with, there was a strong feeling in Israel that not enough effort had been made to find the Nazi criminals, or to punish them. It behooved the Jewish state, therefore, to take the law into its own hands, on behalf of its population, so many thousands of whom were direct victims of Nazi brutality and of the plans Eichmann had helped to make and implement. David Ben-Gurion also wanted the world to know what had really taken place in the Nazi death camps, and how it had happened that six million Jews were slaughtered in Europe. Ben-Gurion and the government of Israel saw the Eichmann trial as more than an act of historical justice. They saw it primarily as a way of teaching the youth of Israel something of the real facts and figures of the Nazi holocaust, and what the component parts of the all but ungraspable evil had actually been. "We must teach the children what happened there," Ben-Gurion said.

The lesson was a long and dreadful one; the trial, which opened in April of 1961, lasted for weeks. It took place in a specially prepared and heavily guarded courthouse in Jerusalem. Day after day, their faces drained of color, the witnesses tremblingly took the stand to narrate what had happened to them, to tell what they themselves had seen, and what they knew, at first hand, of Eichmann's role in the almost successful liquidation of the Jewish people. The trial was broadcast daily, and the meticulously documented case of the prosecution unfolded before the horrified eyes and ears of the Israelis. Like Massada, everyone had been familiar with the contours of the story, and now its separate parts were pieced together in a frightful mosaic.

Adolph Eichmann himself, seated in his bullet-proof glass dock, gazed out at the battery of lawyers and clerks, and at the pale spectators themselves, like an automaton. Politely he answered all the questions in Teutonic monosyllables: *"Ya," "Nein";* imperturbably, he listened to ordinary people relate the hair-raising stories of his complicity in the murder of millions of Jews; without a change of expression, he heard the inevitable verdict handed down.

The hot summer of the trial ended at last. Exhausted, shaken, and relieved, the people of Israel went back to normal life. On May 31, 1962, two years after he had been caught, Adolph Eichmann was hanged in a small prison not far from Tel Aviv. His body was cremated and his ashes scattered at sea. The trial had attracted the attention of the entire world, and brought scores of journalists to Jerusalem. Its pros and cons were to form the subject of many books and legal analyses. But none of these had been its main aim. Its real significance was that Israel had paid respect to the memory of its martyrs, and had brought before its courts a man who had sinned deeply against humanity.

Although unbearably painful for thousands of people, the trial taught other thousands something they had never known before. Jews from Egypt, Yemen, Morocco, and Iraq, for whom Hitler had never been a reality, now understood the dimensions of the disaster that had befallen European Jewry. Eichmann served, ironically enough, to bring together, in retrospective suffering, the very people he had tried so hard to wipe from the face of the earth.

One other major turn of events had great impact on the state during these formative years. This was the involvement of Israel, and of her young agricultural instructors, doctors, nurses, and teachers, with the emerging states of Africa and Asia. In a way, this too might have been anticipated. It was quite natural, after all, that the Jews of Israel, who had learned so much about how to get the best results from the most meager resources, and who had become so effective under such difficult conditions, should be both able and eager to hand their hard-earned know-how on to others. Had there been peace in the Middle East, the neighboring Arab states would have been the obvious beneficiaries of Israel's own experience. As it was, the Israelis became mentors to a dozen brand-new African and Asian states.

In point of fact, they had more to offer than anyone else. While the great powers of the world sent money and heavy equipment as birthday presents to Tanzania, Ghana, and Burma, to the Congo and to Senegal, Israel sent her people. All through the late 1950's and the 1960's, the warm-hearted, successful two-way traffic went on.

From all over Africa, professional delegations and individual students came to study at Israeli hospitals, universities, and agricultural colleges. Hebrew became a bridge, the language that a young English-speaking nurse from Nigeria, working at the Hadassah hospital in Jerusalem, used when she wanted to talk to a French-speaking boy from the Ivory Coast studying veterinary medicine in Rehovoth. The tall, handsome paratrooper training with Israel's Paratroop Corps found that Israel had no color bar at all, and that many Israelis who had come from Arab lands had fairly dark skins themselves. The would-be pharmacists, poultrymen, and research scientists from Sierra Leone, Tanganyika, and Dahomey felt more at home in Israel than in most other places because the Israelis had no colonial past and perfectly understood the perils of discrimination.

But also, Israelis went off by the hundreds to Africa and Asia. They took their families, their textbooks, and their enthusiasm with them. They settled in the toughest, often most out-of-the-way places, and became part of the local scene wherever they landed. They complained less about poor living conditions, about the heat, and about unfamiliar food than most other non-native guests, with the exception of the missionaries. They learned African folk songs and dances, and taught their own to the Africans. Their theme song was a catchy little Israeli tune, "We have brought peace to you," and eventually there was hardly a capital in any of the new African states without an Israeli "Peace Corps" of its own, long before the United States Peace Corps set out on the same path. From one coast of Africa to the other, the Israelis made their mark. They built hotels, schools, and public administration buildings. They set up and manned eye clinics where no eye clinics had ever existed before; they explained about kibbutzim, cooperative villages, and sound banking principles without ever seeming to get weary or bored.

Pioneering was what they knew best, and they couldn't wait to pass the good word on. Here and there, of course, communications sometimes broke down; now and then, plans went awry. But in the main, the experiment succeeded beyond anyone's wildest dreams, and more and more African and Asian countries opened embassies and consulates in · Israel and asked for official Israeli representation back home.

Some of the special Israeli creations were also attractive elsewhere. One of the most popular of these were the pioneer youth movements, patterned after Israel's *Nahal* (from the initials of the Hebrew words for "Pioneer Fighting Youth"). Nahal, operated by the Israel Defense Force, combined military service with work on the land. Eighteen-year-olds, opting for Nahal rather than ordinary military service, spent their first few months doing intensive military training as a group. Then they were transferred to a veteran kibbutz, each group remaining together to get used to life in a collective settlement. Finally, each group was sent out both to farm and guard a frontier settlement, mostly in mountainous or desert areas which were considered too exposed for civilian settlement. Twelve African states and several Latin American countries thought Nahal well worth copying, and Israeli instructors went out to set up the units and stay with them during their first years.

One of the chief by-products of this exciting cooperation was that Israelis found a new outlet for their boundless energy. The developing nations of Africa and Asia gave them a chance to broaden their horizons and feel less cooped up at home. They partially made up for the Arab hostility which adamantly ringed Israel, and they brought about a cultural exchange on a working basis.

In 1961, the millionth newcomer arrived to settle in Israel. Most Israelis were too busy to acknowledge the milestone formally, but though it went uncelebrated, in a sense it marked the coming of age of the state. Life was not particularly easy in Israel—but no longer was it especially hard. Although a third war lay ahead, everyone hoped that the lull in border incursions heralded a real peace, and was overjoyed that the Middle East seemed to be calming down. Then, in the spring of 1967, the skies darkened ominously, and peace fled again.

CHAPTER THIRTEEN

The Six Day War

In May, 1967, Israel turned nineteen. Independence Day that year, as every year before, was greeted by street dancing and fireworks. A new hit song had emerged as the result of the annual song contest marking the state's birthday; it was called "Jerusalem the Golden," and had a charming melody. Although no one knew this in May, it would become the hit song of the Six Day War, and its words were prophetic. Nineteen wasn't very old, but it was, Israelis agreed, a respectable age, and the festivities were gay.

Independence Day, 1967, fell on a Monday. Hundreds of people went up to Jerusalem to watch the modest military parade through the streets of the New City. Others celebrated in less strenuous ways. There was a special concert by the Israel Philharmonic Orchestra, and a gala performance of the Israel National Opera Company, itself now a ripe nineteen years old. Music played a major role in the state's cultural life, and the Philharmonic, whose first concert had been conducted in Tel Aviv in the stormy 1930's by Arturo Toscanini, already had over 36,000 subscribers—an impressive percentage of the total population of two and a half million.

Others went to the theater: that year, over three million tickets to plays had been sold during the eleven-month sea-son. Israel's five repertory theaters and a cluster of small experimental dramatic groups still traveled throughout the country at regular intervals, as they had done in the early pioneering days, and they brought classical drama, ranging from Euripides to Shakespeare, musical comedies such as *My Fair Lady* and *The Fiddler on the Roof,* and the latest works of young Israeli playwrights to every town and large kibbutz from north to south. Most of the plays written by local dramatists dealt with local problems, such as the conflict between the generations in a country of immigration. But the longest lines at any box office that day were for a new Israeli musical called *The King and the Cobbler,* the hero of which was King Solomon.

Another favorite indoor activity was reading. Each year, some 2,000 books rolled off the presses, many of them translations of American and European best-sellers, but many were the works of Israeli writers whose mother tongue was Hebrew. Only a few months earlier, Israel had won her first Nobel Prize: the Nobel Prize for Literature, awarded to Shmuel Yosef Agnon. His mystical stories, dealing with Jewish life in Eastern Europe and with the early Zionist settlements in Palestine, had become famous, translated from Hebrew, throughout the world. Scores of lesser known, younger authors and poets wrestled vigorously with the provocative problem of transforming an ancient tongue into a highly polished and sophisticated instrument of scholarship and literature, and the public avidly read everything that they wrote.

At all events, whether they browsed in museums, got in the car for a day's outing, or just stayed at home with a book, most Israelis celebrated that Independence Day in a justifiably good mood.

One small cloud hovered over the bright horizon—Egyptian troops had suddenly started to move up into the Sinai Peninsula. Cairo's official, though false, explanation was that Israel had threatened Syria, and that, since the two Arab states were bound by a mutual defense pact, Egypt was

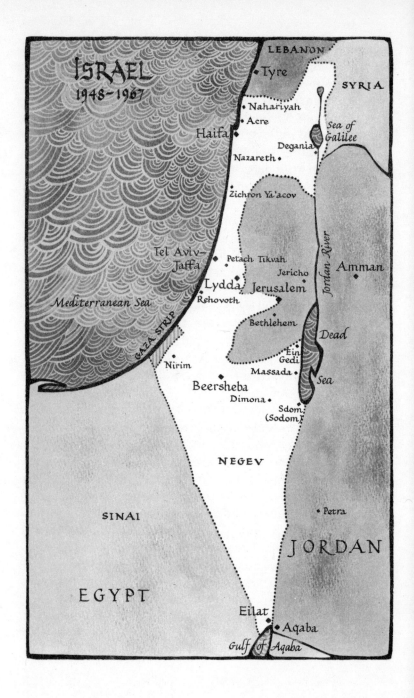

responding to Syria's plight. On the sixteenth of May, Egypt's president, Gamal Abdel Nasser, demanded that the United Nations remove its small Emergency Force from the Israel-Egyptian border at once. This force, made up of a few hundred soldiers, had been posted on the frontiers ever since the Sinai War, and its withdrawal had never been suggested before. In the same breath, and with the same belligerence, the Egyptian president also announced the start of an Egyptian blockade of the Strait of Tiran, at the southernmost end of the Sinai Peninsula, from which all shipping in the Gulf of Aqaba was controlled.

The Israelis were worried, but at first they felt that Nasser's bluster need not be taken too seriously. To begin with, it was very unlikely that the United Nations would indeed tell its police force to withdraw, and secondly, it must be clear to Nasser that closing the Strait of Tiran to Israeli shipping was tantamount to declaring war. But the United Nations' blue and white flag was hauled down at a handful of check posts in the Gaza Strip and at Sharm el Sheikh, which guarded the Strait of Tiran, and the United Nations Emergency Force, bowing to Nasser's demand, got ready to leave the borders of Israel.

The great powers frowned, and hastened to issue anxious statements. British and American warships in the Mediterranean were put on the alert, and the Security Council met in urgent session in New York. The shadow of war, a war which might well escalate into a global conflagration, fell over the Middle East. In Cairo, jubilant crowds demonstrated with hysterical joy at the possibility of an easy attack on Israel, and prayed aloud for victory. This time, said the leaders of the Arab world, Israel would be totally destroyed. Never mind the defeats of 1948 and 1956. Times had changed and the Arabs would now annihilate the Jewish state.

There was some justification for this wishful thinking. Times had indeed changed. For years, the Soviet Union had poured arms and ammunition into the Arab states, had

157

showered them with equipment and with technicians. Egyptian airfields were crowded with the newest Soviet planes, and Russian-made trucks rolled up and down the Sinai Peninsula. Soviet instructors had taken over a large part of the training of the huge Egyptian army, and, presumably, had improved and strengthened it. Hundreds of thousands of Egyptians were under arms in May of 1967, and the Russians assured Cairo that there was more materiel to come. Although the great powers had guaranteed freedom of shipping in the Gulf of Aqaba when they had forced the Israelis to withdraw from Sinai in 1956, now, despite solemn announcements that they would ensure peace in the Middle East, not much seemed to be happening to implement the guarantee. Israel called for partial mobilization, and as the last week of May drew to an unhappy close, the Jewish state began to prepare for what seemed to be inevitable. In Israel, too, people were aware that times had changed. The peril of air raids was infinitely greater than it had been in the two wars through which Israel had lived before. Shops advertised blackout kits and sold tiny plastic identity tags which mothers anxiously tied around the necks of their small children. Householders set about digging trenches in backyards and gardens. The whole country started to clear out its cellars and basements and turn them into air-raid shelters. Mounds of sand were carted to village squares and to main points in all the cities, and schoolchildren, in relays, filled sandbags as some protection against bomb blast.

No one stopped going to work, or abandoned the fields and the spring crops. Children were not kept home from school. But, by the end of May, everyone realized that the worst was not far off. Everywhere, without fanfare or excitement, young men slipped off to join their army units. In the deserts of the south, thousands of Israeli soldiers waited for the enemy to strike. They waited under giant camouflage nets, training and retraining, cleaning gear, and loyally eating cakes baked in the thousands by wives, mothers, and daughters at home.

They gazed at the deep-blue skies and wondered when the first waves of Egyptian bombers would cross the desert. They hoped that if there were indeed to be a war, it would start soon, and the tension of sweating it out in the blistering Negev would end.

By the thirtieth of May, Israelis looked strained and tired. Shops and factories were beginning to feel the pinch of the mobilization, and there were not enough men left in civilian life to bring in the harvests. The morning papers announced that Jordan's King Hussein had signed an anti-Israel pact with President Nasser. Israelis sighed, and prepared to face still another enemy. King Hussein had waited for days for some meaningful support for Israel to come from the great powers, some declaration of their intent to honor the 1957 guarantees, some demonstration that they would try to stop Nasser from carrying out his threats of total war, but the pro-Israel support had not materialized. Egyptian pressure on Hussein was enormous, and at last, he succumbed to it. Losing his nerve, the king flew to Cairo and was folded, literally, into Nasser's embrace.

The clock ticked on mercilessly, each hour bringing Israel closer to the final trial. On the second of June, troops from Algeria and Kuwait entered Egypt, and troops from Iraq and Saudi Arabia joined forces with Jordan's Arab Legion. Israel was now surrounded on all sides. Her hope for survival lay largely in intangibles—in the ability and dedication of her young soldiers, in the talent of her military leadership, and in her determination to fight for her life. In the past, these attributes had compensated for the disproportion in manpower and in equipment. The question was, Would they still suffice against the vast armies and the air armadas now marshaled for an all-out attack against her?

Israelis sat glued to their radios, read their papers over and over again, consoled themselves with the traditional thought that, in any case, there was no alternative, and remembered that in 1940 Britain had stuck it out alone—and had stayed alive. The most cheering single thing that happened in Israel during those days of waiting and suspense was the appointment of General Moshe Dayan as Israel's Minister of Defense. Born and bred in an Israeli village, and now in his early fifties, Dayan had been Chief of Staff during the Sinai Campaign. Israelis are not given to sentimentality or hero-worship, but Dayan was regarded as a man who knew the enemy well, and who would know how to deal with them. Cocky, fearless, and possessed of immense personal magnetism, this one-eyed soldier had the nation's complete confidence. So did the curly-haired Chief of Staff, General Yitzhak Rabin, and, what was perhaps even more important, so did the army. The entire country knew, with a profound sense of gratitude, that the young men impatiently waiting in the scorching desert would die, if need be, in Israel's defense.

Israel's Foreign Minister flew the rounds of the world's capitals, ceaselessly explaining the extent of Israel's peril, and pleading for support. If necessary, Israel would fight, but perhaps war could somehow, after all, be averted. Surely, at zero hour, Israel's friends could intervene to stave off the clash of arms. But nothing happened, no one could or would halt the onrush of events. Public opinion, in the main, was on the side of the Israelis, but no one was willing to take any decisive action against the Arab states.

On the third of June, General Moshe Dayan made his first public appearance as Minister of Defense. He spoke at a press conference in Tel Aviv. He talked calmly, though sadly, about the lessening chances for a diplomatic solution. It was too late, he said, for any kind of military response to the Egyptian blockade of the Strait of Tiran, but too early to arrive at any conclusion about the results of Israel's feverish attempts to secure some sort of political action against the Arabs. The hundreds of journalists who had descended on Israel during the waning days of May decided that although war might not be indefinitely postponed, it was certainly not imminent. Over the weekend, the streets of Tel Aviv,

Jerusalem, and Beersheba filled with young men again. On Israel's beaches, thousands of tanned, tired soldiers stretched out, relaxing, on leave. Israel seemed suddenly to have returned to normal.

But, unknown to most of the population, preparations were still being made for the grimmest eventualities. Attracting no attention at all, rabbis strolled through Tel Aviv's parks, whispering the words which consecrated the playgrounds and shady corners as Jewish cemeteries; and thus made way for the burial, if necessary, of some 60,000 Israelis. With equal discretion, hotels and public halls were prepared as massive first-aid centers, while hundreds of thousands of wooden planks were secretly ordered for making coffins. But all this was kept from public view, and on Saturday, June 3, most Israelis who were not in the army managed to relax a bit, in between listening to news bulletins and donating blood.

By way of contrast, on the same day, an order of the day was issued by the Egyptian Commander in Chief to his troops in Sinai. It read in part: "The results of this . . . moment are of historic importance for the Arab nation and for the Holy War, through which you will restore the rights of the Arabs . . . and reconquer the plundered soil of Palestine."

On the morning of Monday, June 5, Israelis, listening to the 6 A.M. early news broadcast, learned that the enemy had at last moved toward Israeli territory. All through that long day, they heard only the sparsest of news bulletins, informing them that the enemy had been met and engaged at various points. There were no other programs on the air at all; only the brief, unsatisfying communiques, and Israeli music.

At 8 A.M., the first air-raid siren shrieked, and everyone filed into the nearest shelter. Overhead, planes zoomed through the air, the needle-nosed Mysteres and the arrow-like Mirages, each sounding its own characteristic supersonic whine as it sliced the sky. After a while, the sound of planes died down, and everyone left the shelters and went to work.

The war had begun, but none of the civilians in Israel were to learn much about it until later that night. During the morning, General Moshe Dayan broadcast a short and moving message to the troops. "We are a small nation but a brave one," he said. Throughout the day, the radio transmitted the code names of various units that were being called up. "Peace and Greetings," "The Last of the Just," and "Close Shave" were some of the names monotonously repeated each hour on the hour. Most teenagers were out of school by now, and they spent the day delivering mail, digging ditches, and waiting in the corridors of hospitals where they were posted for possible use as stretcher bearers.

Although the public at large still did not know it, in some respects the war had already swung heavily in Israel's favor by the time the first air-raid alarm was over. At 7:45 A.M. on the fifth of June, the first deadly wave of Israeli aircraft was already en route, loaded with bombs and rockets, making for Egypt's air fields. Flying at dangerously low altitudes to avoid Egyptian radar, Israel's planes, in a giant synchronized attack directed against a total of fourteen Egyptian bases, destroyed or maimed the greater part of the Egyptian air force in less than three hours. Some 300 Egyptian planes were smashed on their own home ground. At 11 A.M., General Mordechai Hod, the third-generation sabra who headed Israel's air force, reported to General Dayan: "I am sure not a single bomber is left in Egypt." Relying on first-rate training, on the element of surprise, and on sheer technical competence, Israel had dared leave her own skies virtually unprotected for some 170 minutes in order to achieve one of the most brilliant air victories in history.

The pre-emptive counterattack had shattered Arab air power, and now Israel's mailed fist closed to deliver a mighty blow to Egypt's land forces. Rank upon rank of Israeli armor hammered its way through the Egyptian tank concentrations dug in throughout Sinai. Facing seven Egyptian divisions, three self-contained Israeli divisions moved out to grapple with the enemy. On this battle in the desert depended Israel's future. The order given to the Israeli tank corps was a harsh one: the battle must be fought, with no retreat and all objectives taken, regardless of the cost in casualties. Once again, it was victory or death, not only for the individual soldiers, but for the nation.

By the end of the first day of the Six Day War, Israeli armor had penetrated deep into Sinai and was on the outskirts of Gaza. In the meantime, as the clock raced on, Jordan, miscalculating once again and ignoring Israel's appeals that she stay clear of the conflict, opened an attack on Jerusalem, and heavily shelled Israeli villages along the long Jordanian border. Israel now turned her attention to the central front, and dealt, as she had warned she would, with King Hussein's army. From Radio Amman, the King broadcast to his people: "The hour of our revenge has come." The mailed fist swung hard at the Arab Legion, and Israeli forces ruthlessly pushed the Jordanians back, taking strongpoints north and east of the Old City of Jerusalem, which had been in Jordanian hands since 1948.

By the seventh of June, the Israelis, sweeping forward on all fronts, and fighting with almost inhuman tenacity, continued to mop up the crumbling Egyptian resistance in Sinai, had reached Sharm el Sheikh and taken it, and had returned Syrian fire intended to destroy the kibbutzim that lay directly below the plateau of the Golan Heights.

At home, all attention riveted on the radio, Israelis listened to the evening's nine o'clock broadcast. The first item brought tears to their eyes, tears of thankfulness and of emotion too deep for definition. "The Old City of Jerusalem is in our hands," said the announcer, his voice breaking.

The war had not been fought for any prize, certainly not for territory. But in the Old City of Jerusalem Solomon's Temple had been built, and there, though Jews had been banned from it for nineteen years, its sole relic still stood—the Wailing Wall, called in Hebrew the *Kotel Ha-maaravi,* or the "Western Wall." Once it had been a retaining wall of the Temple courtyard; for generations afterwards Jews had prayed before it and, weeping, had mourned Jerusalem's destruction by the Romans.

Now the pent-up longing of Israel for the Old City burst its bounds. The battle itself had been hard and bloody, much of it waged in hand-to-hand fighting. But, although the casualties were heavy and the wounded were many, the Arab Legion had been repulsed. At two o'clock that Wednesday afternoon, General Moshe Dayan, accompanied by the Chief of Staff and by the commanding officer of the central front, went to the Wailing Wall. In accordance with ancient Jewish tradition, he scribbled a prayer on a scrap of paper and slipped it gently between the sun-warmed stones. It read: "Let peace come to Israel." Around him, jostling onlookers sang "Jerusalem the Golden," and the Army officers joined in the refrain: "Jerusalem of gold, of copper, and of light. For all thy songs, I shall be thy lyre."

An hour or so later, while bearded Orthodox Jews and soldiers fresh from battle linked arms to dance ecstatically before the Wall, General Dayan spoke to the nation. "We have returned to our holiest of holy places. We shall never part with it again," he said. Before the sun set that day, Bethlehem and Hebron, in fact all of the west bank of the Jordan, taken over by the Jordanians after the 1948 War of Independence, was in Israeli hands. At the expense of many lives, great care had been taken not to damage any of the Christian and Moslem holy places. No fire was directed toward the town in which Jesus had been born twenty centuries ago, and Bethlehem offered no resistance to the Israel Defense Forces.

Jerusalem was one city again, and all Israel rejoiced. But the crucial week was not yet over. On June 8, the Israeli army reached and took up positions along the Suez Canal. The desert behind it was stained with blood and marred by the burnt hulks of hundreds of Egyptian tanks. As in the

Sinai Campaign, the booty was too great to be counted. Months after the war, Israelis were still assembling and sorting it—guns, trucks, ammunition, and, most startling of all, the great Soviet ground-to-air missiles which had been given to Egypt but which had never been fired. Now, as had happened in the Sinai Campaign, thousands of thirsty, dazed Egyptian soldiers stumbled barefoot through the wilderness; there were far too many, once again, to be taken prisoner. Israeli army helicopters dropped water to them, and the wounded were tended, but the desert reeked with the smell of death for many weeks.

Only three days had gone by since the Egyptians first moved against Israel. On June 8, Israel dealt with the third and final front—with Syria. This was the one part of the Six Day War the Israeli's fought with any feeling other than that they were doing what had to be done. Of all the Arab states, the Syrians had been the most implacable in their hostility to Israel, the most ferocious in their attacks on Jewish settlements, and the most barbaric in their treatment of Israelis who strayed across the border or were taken prisoner. It was therefore with some measure of real hatred that the Israelis now readied themselves to knock Syria out of the war which she had been largely instrumental in starting.

The battlefield was high above Israel, on slopes seeded with mines, scarred by vast barbed wire entanglements and rendered almost impregnable by trenches and bunkers built by the Russians to withstand relentless pounding. Inching up the steep sides of the Golan foothills, Israelis in bulldozers painfully cleared the way for tanks, paying a terrible toll for their heroism. The war against Syria lasted for only twenty-four hours. By the time dawn broke on the ninth of June, the Israelis had taken the Golan Heights, and the Syrians had fled. For the first time since the state was established, the settlers around the Sea of Galilee were able to plough and to let their children play outside, free from fear and the need for ceaseless vigilance.

The Six Day War was over by the tenth of June. Israel now controlled an area three times her size. Her troops held the crest of the Syrian Heights, the West Bank of the Jordan (whose Biblical place names of Judea and Samaria were at once restored), the Old City of Jerusalem, and all of the Sinai Peninsula. Eight hundred young Israelis had died in those five days. but two and a half million had been saved.

That Saturday scarcely able to realize the speed and scope of the victory, Israelis wondered, often aloud, whether a modern miracle had taken place, and some opened their Bibles and thoughtfully reread the words written two thousand years ago:

"If you say in your heart, 'These nations are more than I and how can I dispossess them?' you shall not fear them but remember what the Lord thy God did unto Pharaoh and unto all Egypt."

CHAPTER FOURTEEN

ISRAEL GROWS UP

EVEN before the Six Day War had completely ended, Israelis, packing themselves into every conceivable sort of vehicle—trucks, buses, cars, bicycles, and even carts—took to the roads to see for themselves what the country looked like, now that its borders had been changed. In part, the unprecedented movement of almost the entire population of Israel from one end of the suddenly expanded land to the other was sightseeing, although on a huge scale. But in part it was also a mass pilgrimage, whose accessories, more often than not, were the lowly picnic basket and a thermos of coffee.

For the first time since the destruction of the Second Temple, the State of Israel and the Land of Israel were one and the same. East Jerusalem, including the Old City, which had formerly been in Jordanian hands, was legally annexed to New Jerusalem, and made one again. The 1,900 years of the separation of the Jews from the City of David were over.

It was therefore to Jerusalem that Israelis streamed first. They came in the hundreds of thousands, all through June, July, August, and September of 1967. Men, women, children, babies carried on backs and pushed in prams, jammed and crowded the Old City. In and out of its alleys they poured—

to the Wailing Wall, and to the Holy Sepulchre; along the Via Dolorosa; in and out of the Old City's dozens of colorful bazaars and markets; up to Mount Scopus and to the lovely Mount of Olives.

Unable to drink in enough of the city's beauty, they came again and again, all summer long. They stood on Temple Mount holding their breath in wonder at the flawless proportions and magnificence of the Dome of the Rock (also known as the Mosque of Omar), where once Abraham had readied his son for sacrifice, where Solomon had built the Temple to house the Holy of Holies, and where, now, the lovely golden dome glinted and gleamed in the sun. Jerusalem was whole again, all of it available, and the Israelis wanted to see, and touch, and be everywhere in it. It was as though, by the density of their presence, they were imprinting themselves on the city again. It was hard to believe, in those first few days, that a war had just ended. Jerusalem turned into a kind of holiday town, and the joy of the Jews was infectious; in their happiness, they were able also to include the enemy, who, only a week before, had sworn to destroy them.

Throughout the Old City, the Arabs, adjusting gingerly to defeat, tried out their first tentative—or long forgotten— Hebrew phrases, called out "Shalom" and, for the most part, smiled back. Then, understanding that the unification of Jerusalem was an accomplished fact, they began to venture out themselves. Like the Jews, they were filled with a curiosity which nothing could contain. Throughout New Jerusalem, groups of Arabs, dressed in their best clothes, marveled, wide-eyed, at the spacious campus of the Hebrew University, at the super-modern Hadassah Hospital, at the Knesset, Israel's parliament, and at the low floodlit pavilions of the Israel Museum. They peered into shop windows and into cafes, puzzled over alterations in the city they had once before shared with the Jews. They visited old friends in the New City; smartly turned out middle-aged Arabs knocked hesitantly on scores of Jewish doors, greeted former colleagues, and spent hours reminiscing. It was like a scene from *Alice's Adventures in Wonderland,* but it was truth, not fiction.

New regulations were issued daily, aligning the two populations. Here and there, Arabs from the Old City sullenly averted their gaze from the rejoicing Israelis; here and there, a shop closed its shutters for good and its owners left for the other side of the Jordan. There were one or two abortive attempts at a general strike in the Old City, and for a while the Arabs refused to open their schools, and lawyers declared they would never practice under the changed conditions. But the Arabs also drove down to Tel Aviv and made for the seashore, and for the zoo, and traveled free of restrictions all over the country.

As in 1948, there were also those who chose to cross the borders, swelling the ranks of Arab refugees in Jordan. But in the main, the two parts of Jerusalem grew together with astonishing rapidity; the Israeli military presence was discreet, and although security measures were firm, they were not obtrusive. The city's deep nineteen-year-old injuries began to heal and the scars of division faded away. By the summer of 1968, it was hard to remember exactly where the ugly barbed wire, the mine fields, and the great concrete barriers had been. It was as though some magnet, embedded deep in Jerusalem, had somehow drawn her people together.

Jerusalem was now the chief center of attraction, but it was far from being the only one. Israelis toured all the new territories, from the snowy slopes of Mount Hermon to the frontier post at Sharm el Sheikh. With unquenchable excitement and interest they stood in line to enter the Tomb of Rachel in Bethlehem and the burial place of the Patriarchs in Hebron. They drove through Nablus and Jericho; went on long, uncomfortable trips through the wilderness of the Sinai Peninsula; and picnicked amid the formidable Syrian fortifications on the Golan Heights. Everywhere, families took the Bible along as a guidebook, showing enthralled children the places from which they had been barred for so long, and everywhere Arab peddlers set up stands and cheerfully sold fruit, Chinese pencils, and British jam to the Jews.

At first, the prospect of managing such large areas, with over one million Arab inhabitants, was a source of considerable anxiety for Israel's Ministry of Defense, which had been charged with the formidable job. But the military governments which were set up based themselves on three principles which turned out to be more successful than anyone might have imagined in the summer of 1967. The first rule established was that the life of the Arabs now under Israel's jurisdiction would be disturbed as little as possible. Other than making sure that their needs, in terms of food, sanitation, and medical treatment, were met promptly, and that they did not harbor terrorists, the Israelis refrained from interfering in the life of the residents of the new territories.

Also, the existing structures of local government remained intact: all of the Arab mayors and heads of villages stayed on in their jobs, and the number of Israeli officials involved in the day-to-day running of the territories was kept to a bare minimum. Thirdly, the Israelis permitted the Arabs total freedom of movement. During the first year after the war, a hundred thousand non-Israeli Arabs went back and forth across the Jordan River; the Gaza Strip, sealed for two decades, was reopened. Moslem pilgrims traveled to and from Mecca, students from universities in the neighboring Arab states came home for holidays and then returned, and families, separated for twenty years, were able to meet again.

It seemed that life had really returned to normal, that now, at last, Israel could settle down. But it was not to be so simple; nothing, it seems, is ever really simple in such a complicated country. The joy of victory and the grief of mourning for those who had fallen in the war were followed by disappointment and shock. Most Israelis had believed that peace was truly in sight, but the leaders of the Arab states remained intransigent. No, they declared, they would not sit down to direct talks with Israel; no, they would not recognize or accept the reality of the State of Israel; no, they would not permit Israeli shipping to use the Suez Canal. They threatened a fourth round of war, and demanded that, before any sort of negotiations started, Israel unconditionally withdraw from all the territories she now occupied.

The Israelis recalled the past. Remembering 1948 and 1956 and 1967, they dug their heels in. This time, they said, representatives of the Arab nations would have to meet face to face with Israelis, thrash out their problems together, and arrive at binding agreements about secure frontiers and the problem of the Arab refugees. Above all, they would have to discuss putting an end to aggression, for the armistice agreements of 1948, which had been designed to lead to peace, had led, instead, to two wars. Israelis looked about them at the new shape of the state, and made up their minds. The farmers facing the Gaza Strip now ploughed their fields safe from daily fear of marauders' bullets; children played happily in the green gardens of the kibbutzim that lay below the Syrian Heights, and at night they slept in their own beds again, not in the familiar underground shelters; Israeli ships sailed through the Gulf of Aqaba undeterred; between Israel and Egypt lay the great expanse of the Sinai Peninsula, across which enemy troops could no longer march with impunity; and on the eastern bank of the Suez Canal, Israeli soldiers maintained constant patrol.

This time, there would be no withdrawal and no return of territory without firm guarantees; no more temporary cease-fire agreements; nothing short of lasting peace. But by the summer of 1968, peace seemed as far away as ever; the Arabs had not changed their minds. Instead, they and their Russian advisors busily trained and armed new bands of infiltrators, saboteurs, and snipers, and each day brought its grim reports of new border incidents and fresh terror. But now, the frontiers of Israel were manageable, and when the toll taken by Arab terrorists mounted beyond endurance, Israel's Defense Forces struck back, deep into enemy territory, wiping out the guerilla encampments which threatened life and property.

It was not peace, nor, on the other hand, was it war. The issues which Israel faced on her twentieth birthday called for infinite patience and strong nerves. One of Israel's young writers defined the situation crisply, in a newspaper article he entitled "No Way Back." Writing in June of 1967, only three weeks after the war was over, he said, "It must be quite plain that not a single Israeli soldier will withdraw from one square meter until and unless the day afterwards, when he has taken his uniform off, he will be free to come back to that same meter of land as an ordinary worker, as a businessman, as a driver, as the captain of a ship—or as a tourist. If the Arab countries decide that there are to be frontiers closed to us, then *we* must retain the prerogative of deciding where those frontiers are to be."

On the second of May, 1968 (as reckoned by the Jewish calendar), Israel, sober, determined, and worried about the future, reached the age of twenty. Her childhood and adolescence had been stormy; her national heritage reached back across a span of two thousand years and included the destruction of six million Jews; her neighbors remained illogically unreconciled to her presence and she still faced the hostility of some of the world's great powers.

The Soviet Union, although chagrined at the failure of the Arabs to exploit the Russian planes, tanks, and arms with which they had been so abundantly provided, was more anxious than ever to gain a firm footing in the Middle East. To this end, therefore, she continued to arm Israel's neighbors and to incite their enmity and aggression toward Israel. France, which only a few years before had gladly supplied Israel with jet planes, financial aid, and other tokens of friendship, now, for reasons of her own, abandoned Israel and turned to woo the Arabs instead. Even a number of African states, recent recipients of Israeli assistance, began to give way before Arab threats, and they, too, joined the

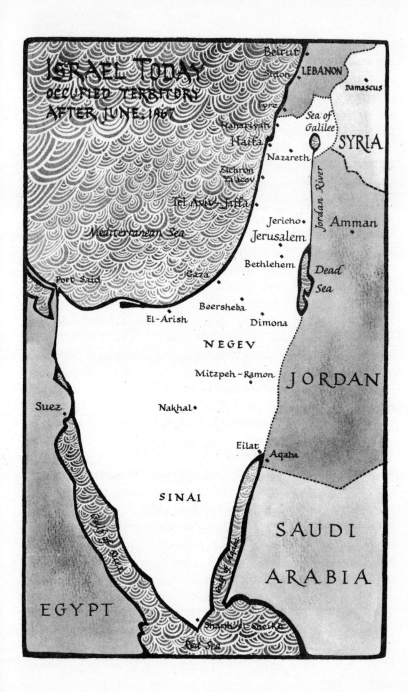

ISRAEL TODAY
OCCUPIED TERRITORY
AFTER JUNE, 1967

Beirut
Sidon   LEBANON
                          Damascus
Tyre
                Sea of
Nahariyah   Galilee   SYRIA
Haifa
        Nazareth
Zichron
Yacov
Tel Aviv~Jaffa
                Jericho   Amman
        Jerusalem
Mediterranean Sea
        Bethlehem   Dead
Port Said   Gaza   Sea
        Beersheba
El~Arish   Dimona
        NEGEV
        Mitzpeh~Ramon   JORDAN
Suez   Nakhal
        Eilat
                Aqaba
        SINAI
                SAUDI

                ARABIA
EGYPT
        Sharm el Sheikh
        Red Sea

Jordan River
Gulf of Suez
Gulf of Aqaba

chorus demanding that Israel withdraw from the new borders whatever the cost.

Staggering under the weight of a massive defense budget, deeply involved in the urgent problems of increasing their water supply, their educational facilities, their housing programs, and, above all, maintaining watch on their frontiers, Israelis pushed away a burgeoning sense of injustice and insecurity, and consoled themselves with the evident understanding and affection of the world's senior democracy, the United States.

Clearly, no force could wipe Israel out. The statistics of the past twenty years were token of her resolve to live, and of the energy and industry of her people.

On the whole, the arithmetic of survival was encouraging. Toted up, the figures which spelled out the rate of Israel's growth were impressive. In 1948, her population numbered 790,000; in 1967, it numbered 2,775,000. In 1949, the cultivated areas of land totaled 412,000 acres; in 1967, they totaled 1,070,000 acres. In 1948, school attendance was 130,000; in 1967, it was up sixfold. In 1949, Israel had exported $35,000,000 worth of goods and services; in 1967, the figure was up twenty-sevenfold.

In whatever direction Israelis looked, they saw the result of their hard work. Industrial production, merchant marine tonnage, highway building, all had doubled and trebled in the twenty years. More importantly, the remarkable venture of Zionism had created an Israeli people, a nation which was still an integral, though a distinctive, part of Jewry throughout the world. The record, in short, warranted optimism.

Young herself, the state boasted of a population that was also young. On her twentieth birthday, the average age of all Israelis was only twenty-nine. They were citizens of a country deeply committed to the future, prepared to sweat out a turbulent present, and constantly aware of the past. Theodor Herzl had called his proposed Jewish state "The Old-New Land," and the name held good in 1968. The crowds that lined the streets of Jerusalem to watch the Independence Day parade on a sunny morning in May of 1968 were more than just residents of a small twentieth-century republic in the restless Middle East. They were, or felt themselves to be, the natural heirs to the land of their forefathers, living threads in a historic tapestry first woven in this same Land some four thousand years ago.

In these ordinary, tired, hopeful people flickered a flame of love for Israel which had first been lit when Abraham, obeying the word of the Lord, led his people into the Promised Land. Then as now, the way had not been easy; then as now, the Jews believed firmly in the special covenant that bound them to this one small country; then as now, believing this, they had no alternative other than to redeem the Land.